my twenty-five years in

FLEETWOOD MAC

HYPERION

NEW YORK

Produced by Larry Vigon Studio

Art Direction: Larry Vigon

Design: Larry Vigon & Brian Jackson

Cover photo courtesy of John McVie

Research: Frank Harding

Photo Editing: Frank Harding & Judy Wong

Project Coordinator: Dennis Dunstan - Wel-Dun Management

Project Coordination, Hyperion: Mary Ann Naples

Special thanks to Lynn Frankel – Big Love from Mick

Photo acknowledgments will be found on page 200

Library of Congress Cataloging-in-Publication Data

Fleetwood, Mick.

My twenty-five years in Fleetwood Mac / Mick Fleetwood :

text by Stephen Davis :

discography by Frank Harding.—1st ed.

p. cm.

Discography: p.

ISBN 1-56262-936-X

1. Fleetwood Mac (Musical Group) 2. Rock Musician—Biography-

3. Fleetwood, Mick, I. Davis, Stephen, 1947- II. Title.

ML421.F57F6 1992

782.42166'09'2—dc20

[B]

First Edition

10   9   8   7   6   5   4   3   2   1

For John McVie
    From the first until this,
the brother I never had you have been to
me. My God, I swear we deserve each other.
    Love you very much ++
            Mick

P.S. Don't you think it's time the
    Freddia took another flight?
I do!!

BEFORE THE BEGINNING

There were times that rang of
innocent energy — A sense Of music
that one by (one we all became part
of That power would be led by Peters
hands in those early days. Looking back, it
was to us all a dream come true.
    Most certainly for myself to this day,
it is the first and last lesson in life and
in music —
        Less is more and more is less

    I hope as we open up, the above makes —
    — Sense.

    Mick

Nothing ordinary ever happened to Fleetwood Mac. In the twenty-five years since "Peter Green's Fleetwood Mac Featuring Jeremy Spencer" made its blistering debut at the Windsor Blues and Jazz Festival on August 13, 1967, the group has been through eleven lineups and has endured every sling and arrow to which bands are prone. Great musicians were lost to madness, drugs, religious ecstasy, jealousy, and exhaustion. At the same time, Fleetwood Mac made some of the most sublime music of its generation, sounds that swayed and inspired millions of fans and eventually reached one of the biggest audiences in history. Fleetwood Mac was *the* archetypal glamour band of the 1970s, that lost, rocket-fueled era of lusty excess and great music. While Led Zeppelin ruled the high school parking lots, and the Eagles had a scruffy elegance of their own, Big Mac really defined the times, and not just the

Peter Allen Greenbaum

Born October 29, 1946 London

(Previous Page) "A couple of weeks before Fleetwood Mac's first gig at the Windsor Jazz & Blues Festival, Peter & I look on from back stage at an open air concert in London. We knew that shortly it was to be our turn." - M.F.

seventies: they were stars in the blues-bustin' late sixties as well as the postmodern eighties, and survive into the nineties, Fleetwood Mac's fourth decade.

Most of us know Fleetwood Mac as the five musicians of its longest (1975-1987) and most spectacular incarnation: Mick Fleetwood, the brilliant long-legged drummer and band leader; John McVie, the taciturn master bassist who was a star even before he joined the band; Christine McVie, the beautiful singer/keyboardist who wrote some of the best songs of our era; Lindsey Buckingham, the intense writer-guitarist who inspired the group to its greatest heights; and the legendary Stevie Nicks, whose white-hot personal magic connected with her audience in a way that went far beyond even that music itself. This was the famous lineup that invented adult rock & roll in 1975 and made an international impact often compared to that of the Beatles a decade earlier. This was the band whose torrid private lives were chronicled in *Rumours*,

"Peter Green, my leader and mentor, indeed the founder of Fleetwood Mac. He's never far away, to this day my favorite guitar player. This is *his* band." - M.F.

their 1977 masterpiece that is still one of the best-selling recordings ever made. And this was the group that transplanted itself to America, hired a struggling L.A. waitress, and turned her into one of the most lustrous stars in the musical heavens.

So here – on its twenty-fifth anniversary – is Fleetwood Mac. Their communal story is a larger-than-life fable of genius and love, failure and success, and artistic triumphs whose influence will be felt for many years still to come. Let us now make a chronotransduction – a passage across time – and recreate the damp London cityscape where the young Fleetwood Mac first flowered, years before they decamped for California sunshine and their place in artistic history of our century.

Fleetwood Mac began life as an outgrowth of English music fans' love for black American blues, which took root when Muddy Waters roared through

1st gig. August 13, 1967 (Windsor Jazz Festival) "What a great way for a band to start out; with people as far as we could see, people that in the short time we played let it be known our first step had been taken, and enjoyed by one and all. In fact the festival was a feast of music unique to that day and age that I will long remember." - M.F.

Britain in 1958.

Until then, British enthusiasts of "trad" jazz (Dixieland in the U.S.) had been content with a homegrown folk-shuffle style called skiffle and occasional tours by American blues musicians – Big Bill Broonzy, Josh White, Sonny Terry, and Brownie McGhee – who played acoustic country blues derived from the Delta plantations of the lower Mississippi.

When Muddy came through in '58, he changed everything and launched a cultural shock wave. Traveling with his pianist, Otis Spann, Waters brought with him an electric guitar and amplifiers instead of the weathered acoustic the English were expecting. Instead of coveralls and straw hats, Muddy and Otis wore suits, dark glasses, glossy pointed boots, and slick, processed hair. Turning up his amps, Muddy blew 'em away with the driving, electronic Chicago R&B. SCREAMING GUITAR AND HOWLING PIANO read the headlines of the music press the following week.

By the early 1960s, London began to sprout R&B bands of its own. Cyril Davies and Alexis Korner were early pioneers: out of their groups

5

sprang the first wave of the
Great British Blues Boom – the
Rolling Stones, Yardbirds, and
John Mayall's Bluesbreakers,
the direct ancestor of
Fleetwood Mac.
Mayall had arrived from
Manchester in 1963 with a
talent for attracting young
players interested in pure
blues. Needing a bass, he
recruited a twenty-year-old
amateur guitarist from Ealing
in western London.
John McVie.
McVie was a trainee tax
inspector who moonlighted in
local groups. Since lots of good
guitarists were around, he
removed the top two strings
from his guitar and started
playing bass. Given a pink
Fender bass by his dad,
inspired by the music of
England's premier band, the
Shadows, McVie joined Mayall
who taught him the rudiments
of twelve-bar blues.
Immediately Mayall discovered
John's natural ability to really
rock a band, and The
Bluesbreakers quickly became
one of the first real
"underground" groups on the
cusp of Swinging London, that
legendary era when music,
fashion, and art took over an

John McVie took his rightful place in the band
three weeks after the Windsor Festival.

entire generation on both sides of the Atlantic. The Bluesbreakers broke out of tedium when Eric Clapton got disgusted with the Yardbirds' attempts at a hit single. Clapton was a bluesman, uninterested in pop success, and in 1964 he accepted Mayall's offer to become a Bluesbreaker. Soon Eric's talent began to inspire graffiti scrawled on subway walls: CLAPTON IS GOD. The London scene in 1964-65 was extremely cross-pollinating. Young musicians jumped in and out of groups, learned and stole from each other, hustled around to make a living. One of the best of these was a teenage butcher's apprentice from the slums of East London who idolized Eric Clapton and was teaching himself to play guitar. Peter Green.

His real name was Peter Greenbaum, from a poor family in Whitechapel. Greenie, as they called him, was both humble and *extremely* charismatic. Ever conscious of his class background, he felt he had a right to sing the blues.

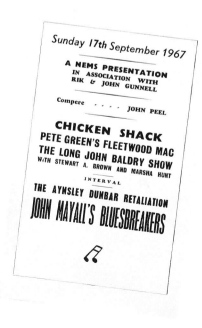

(Above) Peter Green's Fleetwood Mac.
(Below) The band arrive home, from their first American west coast tour of Los Angeles & San Francisco.

He showed genius as soon as he began to play, developing a beautiful tone that became the envy of masters like B.B. King and Jimmy Page. Early on, Peter was a Clapton disciple; he followed the Bluesbreakers around so he could sit at Eric's feet, watching his fingers on the frets. He bought a Gibson Les Paul guitar because Eric played one, and gigged around London with the Tridents and other groups. When Clapton got bored with Mayall and asked to leave, he was replaced temporarily by Peter Green.

Eric returned after a holiday, and Peter found a job with the Peter B's, a London pop group run by a young organist Peter Bardens. Billed as "Cool Blue Pop," the B's played the usual circuit of pubs and clubs dominated by the Marquee and the Flamingo in Soho. The group's drummer was a tall military brat from the country who played simply and steadily and stood out in any crowd.

Mick Fleetwood.

Mick was the son of an RAF war hero. Born in 1947, he grew up abroad, as his father was posted around NATO, then returned to a succession of

Peter Green's Fleetwood Mac's first publicity shot for their record label Blue Horizon.

English boarding schools, where he neglected to study. All he desired was to be a drummer in London's fabled West End. Leaving school at fifteen with a drum kit bought by his parents, he migrated to London, practicing in a garage until "discovered" by Peter Bardens, who lived next door. Mick played in the Cheynes, a short-lived but good mod group, and then in the Peter B's, where he became friends with, and was inspired by, Peter Green.

This group was going nowhere by 1966, so they changed their name to Shotgun Express and hired two singers – Rod Stewart and Beryl Marsden – and plied the northern soul circuit. Soon Peter and Beryl fell in and out of love, and that was the end of that group.

There was also turbulence in the Bluesbreakers. McVie liked to drink, and was often fired by the puritanical Mayall. One of his replacements was Jack Bruce, who got along well with Clapton. When these two left to form Cream, McVie was back in, and so was Peter Green.

(Above) John Mayall and Peter Green in the Bluesbreaker days 1966.

(Below) Peter Green, his girlfriend Sandra Elsdon & John McVie.

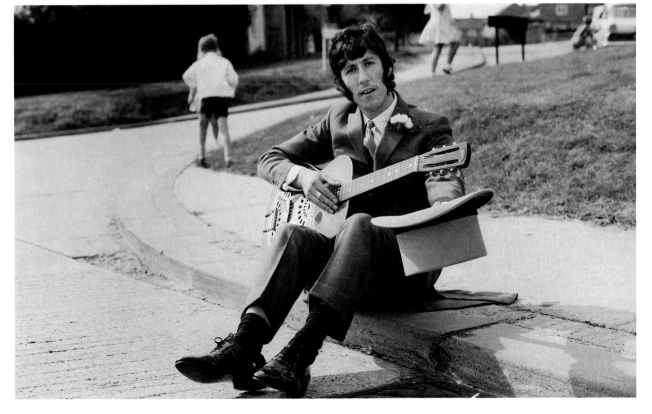

At first, Mayall's fans were furious that Clapton had been relpaced by an unknown. Then Peter Green would start to play, and his deep, spiritual tone was like magic. Soon there was new writing on the walls: PETER GREEN IS BETTER THAN GOD.

From the start, Green displayed a showmanship that cut against the grain of his humble style. Once his position with Mayall was secure, he concentrated on his blues playing, and fans started to refer to him as The Green God. He had a lot to prove after Clapton's performances on Mayall's *Bluesbreakers* album, but his brilliant playing on its successor, *A Hard Road*, established Green as the equal of Clapton, Beck, and Page. Peter's instrumental work on "The Stumble" and "The Supernatural" foreshadow the kind of technically superior, emotionally riveting music that would soon empower the fledgling Fleetwood Mac.

Mick Fleetwood, meanwhile, was trying to make a living painting houses after Shotgun Express died. One day

(Above) John McVie - Bluesbreaker

(Below) Peter Green as best man at a friend's wedding.

Peter Green called and said that Mayall had fired his drummer. Would Mick like the gig? Fleetwood was petrified as he walked into his first gig as a Bluesbreaker. The place was jammed, and the fans began to heckle when they realized the old drummer was gone. Soon McVie had enough. Stepping to the microphone, he told the hecklers, "Why don't you fuck off and listen?" Thus began a friendship that was often cemented by the mutual bending of elbows. Soon Mayall decided that two serious drinkers in the band was one too many. After six weeks, Fleetwood was let go. But the seeds of the new band had already been sown.

While Mick was still a Bluesbreaker, Mayall had given Peter Green some studio time for his birthday. Green, Fleetwood, and McVie cut three songs: "It Hurts Me Too," "Double Trouble," and an untitled instrumental. Mick Fleetwood still remembers Green deciding to name the instrumental after his favorite rhythm section. The name Green scrawled on the tape

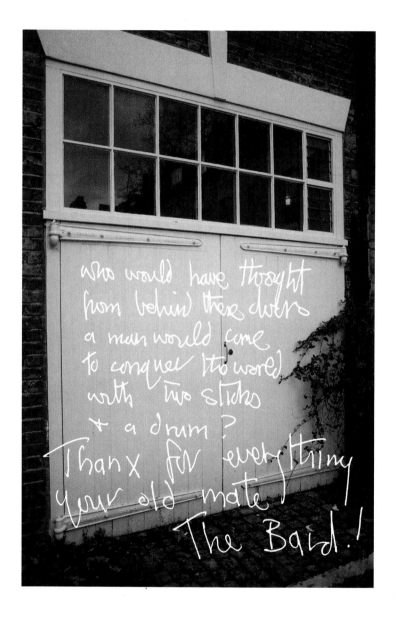

who would have thought from behind there doors a man would come to conquer the world with two sticks + a drum? Thanx for everything your old mate The Band.!

"Peter - Thank God you got me out of the garage." - M.F.

(Far right) Michael John Kells Fleetwood

12

canister was "Fleetwood Mac."
Peter Green left John
Mayall's group in 1967, after
Fleetwood's departure. He was
being courted by the
Bluesbreakers' producer, Mike
Vernon, who wanted to start his
own record label and needed
Peter's magisterial blues
authority as his first act. Peter
asked Mick to join him: that
was the core of the new band.
They asked McVie to join and
were refused! John had been
with Mayall for four years, he
was making good money, and
liked the job security. Green
and Fleetwood were devastated.
Turned down by the best bass
in England! And they were
naming the group – *Fleetwood
Mac* – feeling sure they would
get him. Peter Green was
straightforward and idealistic:
He loathed the role of "guitar
god" that was thrust upon
brilliant colleagues like
Clapton. Peter just wanted a
good blues group with a
minimum of fuss or ego trips. It
was typical of his character to
name his new group after the
rhythm section, not himself.

John Graham McVie poses as a trainee tax
inspector, which was his only other job which
he held for 9 months. He's been a full time
musician ever since.
(Far right) Mick drumming with the
Bluesbreakers.

"Don't worry," he told Fleetwood. "McVie will come over in time. The writing's on the wall."

So Peter placed an ad in *Melody Maker* for a bass player. It was answered by an amateur named Bob Brunning, who showed up at Peter Green's door. "Do you know," Brunning stammered, "about the Peter Green who plays with John Mayall?"

"You bloody idiot! I am Peter Green." Brunning was hired without an audition and was told that the new band's first gig was the prestigious Windsor Jazz and Blues Festival. They would be performing in front of tens of thousands of fans, in two weeks' time.

The new band still wasn't complete. Peter Green informed Vernon that he didn't want to front the band himself. He refused to be the star. So Vernon played him a tape of a Midlands band he'd recorded while scouting the country for his employer, Decca Records. The band, from Lichfield, was terrible, but when Peter Green heard the guitarist he turned very pale and said, "My God."

It was Jeremy Spencer.

Peter Green at Decca's West Hempstead Studios, London 1966.

Jeremy was a five-foot blues hellion with a fifteen-year-old wife and a baby, and he played his big Gibson like Elmore James resurrected. He sang Elmore's songs – "Dust My Broom," "Madison Blues" – like he'd just stepped off a bus from Arkansas. It was a brilliant act, way beyond mere imitation, more on the level of re-created art. Peter went north to hear him play: On his return he announced to Vernon that the new band would be billed as Peter Green's Fleetwood Mac Featuring Jeremy Spencer.

The band rehearsed a bit, and debuted at Windsor in August 1967. It was a Sunday night finale headlined by Cream, the new Jeff Beck Group, and Mayall. Mick Fleetwood was petrified. This was their first gig, in front of thirty thousand fans. Peter Green motioned Bob Brunning to the mike to announce the first song. Brunning was so scared he forgot the name of the tune. Just then Jeremy blasted the clarion heavy metal "Dust My Broom" lick, and the crowd went wild. Then Peter took over. Liberated by Jeremy's act, he had the

Peter Green's Fleetwood Mac

(Below) Peter Green & Jeremy Spencer.

freedom to craft globular, pulsating runs that communicated intense feeling to the audience, who in turn responded with waves of applause and cheers. Fleetwood Mac's set only lasted twenty minutes. Halfway through, Mick Fleetwood knew he was in something ready to explode.

After the gig, they saw John McVie backstage, waiting to go on with Mayall. They pleaded with him to join the band. Look, they begged John, we've named the group after you! Still, McVie refused. He finally joined the band three weeks later in September 1967, at which point Fleetwood Mac began to earn its reputation as a fire-breathing blues dragon.

By 1968, Fleetwood Mac was being called the best live band in England. Now it was time to record. The group's first sessions were piratical

Mike Vernon, co-founder of Fleetwood Mac's first record label, Blue Horizon. "Mike Vernon, the initial person to give Fleetwood Mac support and recognition by making us the first band to be signed to Blue Horizon. The relatively short time that we spent on Blue Horizon was to be the band's most prolific period." - M.F.

(Below) Clifford Davis, Fleetwood Mac's first manager.

(Far right) The back cover of "The Original Fleetwood Mac" album.

after-hours raids on Decca's West Hampstead studio, to which Mike Vernon had a key. These demos were intended to get both the band and Vernon's new label, Blue Horizon Records, a deal. The group was quickly signed by Columbia's British subsidiary, CBS. The first album, *Peter Green's Fleetwood Mac*, was basically the band's live show, recorded in only three days. It was an instant smash, spending seventeen weeks on the charts, rising to number four. There was a flurry of Macmania, with people actually fighting to get into the still small gigs. Their first single was Jeremy's version of the Jamesian "I Believe My Time Ain't Long." Peter's mellow "Ramblin' Pony" blues was on the flip side. Soon Fleetwood Mac began to tire of their role as high priests of British Blues. Groups like Cream and the Jimi Hendrix Experience were stretching the blues format into new worlds of psychedelia and feedback. Meanwhile, Fleetwood Mac was urged by its fans to stay true to Chicago-style R&B. The group, goaded

Fleetwood Mac on their second U.S. Tour. Grand Ballroom, Detroit. December 26, 1968 (Far right) "While in Detroit, Peter Green sent this to ex-Bass player Bob Brunning." - M.F.

Hallo Folks

Thanks for buying all those copies of Albatross. Christmas Eve here and snowing outside. my hotel room is very hot though. Everywhere except New York a huge success so far (New York was our first gig and we had problems with it.) Wish I was there, Honest! In Detroit right now, not the kind of place to spend Christmas at all. Happy new year!! I love you all. Peter Greenbaum.

Lusterchrome REG. U.S. PAT. OFF. MADE ONLY BY TICHNOR BROS., INC., BOSTON 15, MASS.

Dahlia (Mixed Colors)

POST·CARD

Mr & Mrs Brunning & Simon.
8 Bullen St.
Battersea.
LONDON
ENGLAND.

by the satyr-like Jeremy, responded by alternating R&B with obscene vaudeville pranks involving condoms filled with milk or beer and tied to tuning pegs then tossed into the audience; a huge pink dildo named Harold that was mounted on Fleetwood's bass drum; and dirty language that finally got them banned from the Marquee, which might have killed a lesser group.

Still needing a hit single, Peter Green wrote "Black Magic Woman" in early 1968. The song failed for Fleetwood Mac, but in time became a hit for Carlos Santana, a young San Francisco guitarist the group met on its first visit to America later that year. (They literally watched as Santana auditioned for an opener slot in one of Bill Graham's shows at the Winterland Ballroom.) Meanwhile, between trips to Mac strongholds like Germany and Scandinavia, the group honed its blues while working as Blue Horizon's house band, backing visiting legends B.B. King and Otis Spann.

In mid-1968, Fleetwood

Uddersucker

"An album cover that didn't make it!"   - M.F.

(Far left) Mr. Wonderful

"An album cover that did."   - M.F.

Mac recorded its second album, *Mr. Wonderful*, in London. This marked the band's first collaboration with a beautiful young pianist Mike Vernon had brought to the session: Christine Perfect. She was from Birmingham, in the Midlands, the daughter of a professor and a woman who had a talent for healing people. The family was musical and artistic, and Chris was a university-trained sculptress who was part of a college music scene that spawned the Spencer Davis Group, featuring that whiskey-voiced teenager Steve Winwood. Soon Chris joined Chicken Shack, a bluesy group that played the same circuit as Fleetwood Mac, who all lusted mightily after her. She chose the charming McVie; they married that summer, in part to please Chris's terminally ill mum. The newlyweds spent their first year of marriage on the road, with different bands. Christine Perfect, winner of *Melody Maker's* Best Female Singer award in both 1968 and 1969, then became known as Christine McVie, and retired from a promising career.

Fleetwood Mac as a four piece.

(Far right) Tour poster for 1968 Scandinavian tour.

SBA and
Clifford
Davis
present:
**FLEETWOOD
MAC IN
CONCERT**

THEN PLAY ON

These times were short lived, and yet the making of the album "Then play on" ~~spawned~~ a musical freedom within Fleetwood Mac, that became an anthem, which in my mind has led more often to the very revival of the band.

Indeed many major factors came from this phase of Fleetwood Mac, like the addition of Danny Kirwan who became Peter Green's guitar partner. And as such, musically Fleetwood Mac grew to a five piece, that for the most part would set a precedent of having three performer songwriters ~~within~~ within the ranks of Fleetwood Mac for many years to come.

Another way of explaining the above would be as Shakespeare said, "If music be the food of love then play on"

Now Peter Green became restless. Something was missing. He never wanted to lead the band as its resident star, and Jeremy didn't write songs and was limited as a performer. Peter wanted more help, so he recruited a third guitarist and songwriter: Danny Kirwan. Danny was to Peter as Peter had been to Eric Clapton – an awestruck fan. They met him at one of their regular gigs, the Nags Head pub in Brixton, where Danny came to sit at Peter's feet. Like Peter, Danny was a fluid guitarist in love with vibrato and sustained notes. He had a little band, but was eventually hired for Fleetwood Mac because Peter liked to play with him and thought he could write songs.

Late in 1968, Peter Green tried again for a hit single. The result was "Albatross," recorded just before Fleetwood Mac's second voyage to America. An understated, atmospheric instrumental, "Albatross" was colored by washes of Caribbean pastels and captured a certain

"The rhythm section gets married." - M.F.

(Above) John McVie

(Below) Jenny & Mick Fleetwood

(Previous page) "Enter Danny Kirwan, and then we were five." - M.F.

wistful mood. It was the band's first hit record.

In America Fleetwood Mac – now a quintet – began to take off. They played before a hundred thousand at the Miami Pop Festival. In California they became friends with the Grateful Dead, with whom they would tour. In New York they hunkered down at the Gorham Hotel between gigs at the Fillmore East and nightclubs like Steve Paul's Scene. They plied the ballroom circuit: the Boston Tea Party, Philadelphia's Electric Factory, the Whiskey in Los Angeles. Janis Joplin laughed in the wings of the Fillmore as she watched Jeremy working onstage with Harold the dildo dangling from his fly.

In January 1969, Fleetwood Mac was in Chicago, opening for their hero B.B. King at the famous Regal Theater. Hearing that Chess Records was about to close down its legendary studio, Mike Vernon arranged for the group to record there with some of the city's most venerable blues elders – Willie Dixon, Otis Spann, Honeyboy Edwards, and Walter "Shakey"

(Far left) John McVie

(Above) John & Christine McVie

(Below) Christine McVie

Horton. They were the last blues recordings Fleetwood Mac ever made.

When they returned to England, it was in triumph. They had established themselves in America, and "Albatross" was the number-one record in the country. This haunting song was so influential that the Beatles recorded "Here Comes the Sun King" in honor of Peter Green.

The Green God had won his spurs, but soon they would start to feel like chains.

By 1969, Fleetwood Mac was outselling the Beatles and Rolling Stones in Europe and beginning its conquest of America. The group spent as much time as possible in the U.S., where its record company had declined to release their blues albums. Instead, that year Epic issued a compilation titled *English Rose*, which included "Albatross." This song perfectly fit the new "free form rock" FM stations that were beginning to sprout around America; these would provide Fleetwood Mac with its core audience for the rest of the group's career.

Fleetwood Mac's second U.S. tour - Live at the Electric Factory, Philadelphia, December 1968.

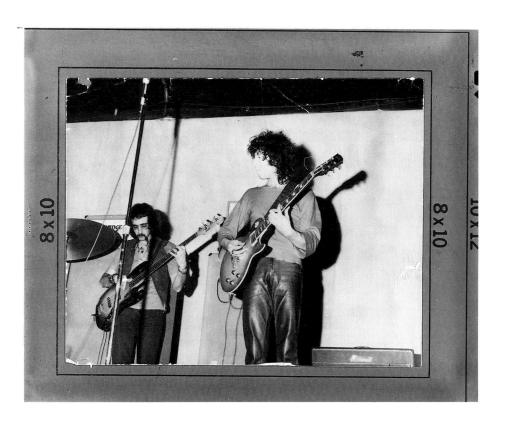

Success brought Peter Green unhappiness, and he gave increasing stage time to Jeremy Spencer, whose gift for mimicry extended to the pioneers of rock & roll. In this period, Fleetwood Mac functioned virtually as the house band of the Boston Tea Party. The second set each night saw Jeremy and Fleetwood Mac mutate into an oldies group, Earl Vince and the Valiants. Jeremy would slick back his hair, don a gold lamé suit the band bought for him, and launch into drunken but hilarious impersonations of Elvis, Little Richard, Jerry Lee Lewis, and Fats Domino. It was rock vaudeville, and the audiences loved it. The band traveled all over the country opening for the Dead. In New Orleans they narrowly missed being arrested in the big acid bust described in the Dead's "Truckin'."

Back in England, Mike Vernon fell out with Fleetwood Mac's manager, Clifford Davis. The Beatles were keen to sign Fleetwood Mac to their new label, Apple Records. They loved the Green God, and Mick Fleetwood was about to marry

Jeremy & Mick

"As always - partners in crime." - M.F.

the beautiful young model
Jenny Boyd, whose older sister
Patti was married to George
Harrison, so there was a family
connection. But, to Peter
Green's dismay, the band's next
single, "Man of the World," was
released in April 1969 by
Andrew Oldham, the Stones'
ex-manager, on his Immediate
label after Oldham bought the
track from Vernon. "Man of the
World" was Peter Green's
introspective, troubling
confession of depression, not
usually the stuff of which hit
singles are made. Nevertheless,
Fleetwood Mac was so big at
the time that the record went to
number two on the English
charts and was a smash in
Europe as well.

Fleetwood Mac's next
album, its last with Peter
Green, was released on its new
label, Warner Brothers, in
September 1969. *Then Play On*
was edited mostly from savage
all-night studio jamming
influenced by the Grateful
Dead's psychedelic anthems,
but also included Pete's
monumental R&B tribute to

(Above) John McVie

(Below) Jeremy Spencer

(Far left) Mick Fleetwood

(Above left) Jeremy and Danny Kirwan

(Below left) Jeremy

masturbation, "Rattlesnake Shake." Jeremy was absent from the record, since the original plan had been to release a simultaneous record by "Earl Vince" – a concept the record company passed on. Danny Kirwan contributed several songs that showed potential, but the album's highlight was a deeply personal and downcast Peter Green composition called "Oh Well" that reflected his disillusionment with his band and the music business. "Oh Well" was great, but it was a downer. When Pete chose it as a single, Mick and John bet him ten pounds it wouldn't even chart. "Oh Well" reached number two in England. But the cost to Fleetwood

---

1971 - Fleetwood Mac headline for Bill Graham "There is so much that has been said about Bill Graham by others. I would like to take this opportunity to tell what the man Bill Graham meant to me and to Fleetwood Mac. Bill, I remember, from the first gig we played made so much effort to make the atmosphere so right, that we just found ourselves wanting to do our very best for the audience. He really did have an incredible hold over the whole proceedings. The amazing point being that his talent in what he did prevailed from the first gig Fleetwood Mac performed through to the very last. Most of all, Bill loved what he did, and that's the reason he will be remembered with love by Fleetwood Mac. Thank You Bill Graham." - M.F. (January 8, 1931 - October 25, 1991)

Mac was the Green God himself. Racked by self-doubt, dabbling heavily in LSD, tormented by royalty statements most musicians would have killed for, Pete went to pieces. He would harangue the other musicians about becoming a charity band, playing in order to give all their money away. It was a most noble idea, Mick told Pete, but could it really work?

Peter Green's valedictory was a single called "The Green Manalishi (With The Two Pronged Crown)." Conceived in a nightmare, he told Mick, the song described a hellish descent into voices, madness, despair. Fired by incendiary guitar playing, it was Pete's way of communicating what had happened to him. It was brilliant, and went to number two on the charts: Fleetwood Mac's fourth straight hit single. (It would be six years before they had another top-thirty record in England.)

By the spring of 1970, it seemed to be the end of the line for the band. Although *Melody Maker* named Fleetwood Mac Best Progressive Group (to the Beatles' Best Pop Group), Peter Green informed the others that he wanted to quit.

Mick tried to talk him out of it, but during a German tour Pete fell in with some rich acid-heads in Munich, and decided to quit the band after previously booked dates had been played. By May 1970, their leader was gone.

Fleetwood Mac almost died when Peter Green left. The remaining musicians were severely demoralized (McVie even talked about being a roadie for a while), and they were scheduled to begin an American tour that autumn. The band was living communally in the Hampshire countryside in a converted oast barn called Kiln House. Musicians, wives, children, and animals were jumbled together, trying to figure their next move. Jeremy and Danny faced fronting the band by themselves, and there was talk of quitting. But Mick Fleetwood refused to concede. "We can't stop now," he told them in meetings that lasted through the summer nights. "If you're a musician, you have to just go on. Let's keep rehearsing! Something good will happen."

(Above) Danny, Mick, John, Jeremy, his wife Fiona & son Dicken.

(Below) John & Christine McVie

36

"As I said at the beginning, every
picture tells a story"
    This one makes me feel like the
moment happened yesterday. Peter,
having made his mind up to leave
Fleetwood Mac left the rest of us hanging
on every gig; knowing, but not wanting to
accept that an era was coming to an end.
    Yes Peter would be gone, and nothing
could change his mind."

MUSICAL CHAIRS

The very phrase "musical chairs" conjures up an atmosphere like the game suggests — you're in, you're out, you're up, you're down.

In other words, compared to those beginning days, Fleetwood Mac would become less focussed, and set out on a musical roller coaster.

Peter Green's influence now gone; left Jeremy, Danny, John and myself feeling a vacuum, to say the least. It was sink or swim, yet we found it but slowly slowly, ways to remain buoyant.

Into that vacuum first came Christine McVie, who from the moment of becoming part of the band injected new creative energy, which grew over the years to become a unique musical style that still to this day is a major part of Fleetwood Mac.

During these times Bob Welch would join the ranks of Fleetwood MAC, adding yet another perspective into the identity of the band. Bob along with John, Christine and me, Mick would ~~see~~ Danny Kirwan leave Fleetwood MAC.

Danny, in my opinion with his sense of melodic harmony, left his mark on me, and for all to hear. Yes, the playing of "musical chairs" was well underway.

Bob Weston and Dave Walker would play their parts as members of Fleetwood MAC, ~~as did~~

Creatively and emotionally these were ~~strange~~ days indeed!

Truly the end of this period came when after the making of the album — — — "Heroes are hard to find" and a long trek on the road, Bob Welch decided to leave the band. I think he was feeling frustrated musically, and certainly professionally with the lack of results.

Bob went on to enjoy great success with his solo career.

"Fate Decides" (one of Bob's songs), seems both to apply to Bob himself and to Fleetwood Mac.

what a strange song!

It turned out Fleetwood Mac's savior was already living with them. Christine McVie was persuaded to come out of retirement and join the band. Her warm, healing alto took the raw edge off Fleetwood Mac and propelled *Kiln House*, the album they undertook to promote on the road in America in September 1970. Christine McVie debuted as Fleetwood Mac's keyboard player and earth mother that month at The Warehouse in New Orleans. FM radio stations were playing *Kiln House*, especially Chris's "Station Man." The tour went well and it looked as though Fleetwood Mac might just survive the loss of the Green God, who had left the music scene (after recording a solo album, *End of the Game*) and was working as a gravedigger.

Back in England, Fleetwood Mac bought themselves an old country house called Benifolds, deep in the Hampshire landscape. The new lineup toured Europe before returning to America again in February 1971.

From the beginning, they all

"To be a four-piece band again was to be shortlived. In fact, this lineup was never to tour. However, we were to make the album 'Kiln House.'" - M.F.

(Page 38) Benifolds. Fleetwood Mac bought this seven-acre rural retreat in Haslemforg, South East England, in early 1971 as a home for the band and their families.

knew something was wrong with Jeremy. The former scatological blues imp had left a new baby at home. He and his young wife Fiona often prayed together, and she had sewn a miniature Bible in the lining of his overcoat to protect him on his travels. Jeremy was a frightened man. Making matters worse, the vibes were really weird when Fleetwood Mac hit California. Los Angeles had been rocked by a terrible earthquake. The sky was yellow and the city stank of ozone and destruction. Jeremy was sitting next to John McVie on the plane descending into LAX. Jeremy looked out the window at still-seismic L.A. and said, "What the hell am I doing here?"

The band checked into the Hollywood Hawaiian prior to their gig at the Whiskey. Jeremy Spencer told his roommate, Mick Fleetwood, that he was going out to visit a bookstore on Hollywood Boulevard.

He never came back.

The rest of the band waited for hours, canceled the show and called the police. Jeremy was listed as missing. They were frantic with worry that their little guitar player had been murdered by Manson's children. The truth wasn't that far away from their worst fantasy.

After a few days, they found Jeremy in a locked and guarded warehouse operated by the Children of God, a hippie-era religious cult that took runaways off the street and sent them off for reprogramming in apocalyptic Christian doctrine. Gone were Jeremy's curly locks and obscene patter, replaced by a shaved head, flowing clothes, and protestation of having found his true path. When asked about his family Jeremy smiled blankly and said that God would look after them. Back at the Hollywood Hawaiian, the scene was disconsolate. The tour, upon which the band's future depended, still had six weeks to run. Jeremy had been half the show. Their manager assured them they were finished if they canceled. No one would ever book them again. So they called Peter Green and begged him to come on the road with them. Astonishingly, he consented. Fully bearded and wearing long caftans, he rejoined the band on a temporary basis on the condition they play non-structured songs. The repertory consisted of endless jams based on "Black Magic Woman," and went down pretty well with the audiences despite Pete's distracted air of contempt and aloofness. The tour actually made money; when it was over, Peter

(Above) The "Kiln House" band
(Below) August 1970, Los Angeles. Christine McVie's first tour with Fleetwood Mac.
(Far right) Danny and John

44

Green quit the band again, saying he'd only wanted to help out his old mates.
The Green God never came back.

Back in their English country seat, the remaining members of Fleetwood Mac – Chris, Mick, John and Danny – were determined to carry on, despite sage professional advice to change their name and style. They needed a great guitar player who could share songwriting chores – and fast. A British tour was booked for June 1971, and the band owed their record company a new album.
They held out hope for a few weeks that Jeremy would rejoin them; he had written to the band, trying to explain his desertion. In the meanwhile, they held auditions for the first time in their history. A couple of dozen guitar players arrived at Benifolds, but none of them stayed. Finally Judy Wong, an old friend of Fleetwood Mac, found their fifth member, whose mystical sound would help guide Fleetwood Mac through the

1968 - Taken in Mick's flat in London: 74 D Kensington High St.
"With Christine now in Fleetwood Mac, it would be the beginning of an onward going marriage that still holds form to this day. There are so many thoughts I have when Chris comes to mind–all of them good. Chris, thank you for keeping your head firmly screwed on throughout the years! I love you, Mick" - M.F.

difficult early 1970s.

His name was Bob Welch.

He was the first American in Fleetwood Mac.

Born in southern California, Bob was a Hollywood kid who joined an Oregon-based integrated soul band – Ivory Hudson & The Harlequins – when he was still in his late teens. This group migrated to Los Angeles and settled into the black club circuit around the time of the 1966 Watts riots. They were a great show band: contemporary stars like Steve McQueen and Muhammad Ali turned out to see them. They also toured Europe, where they played Aretha Franklin's hits in jet-set clubs.

Back in L.A., Welch's band changed its name to the Seven Souls, and lost a crucial battle-of-the-bands (the winner got the record deal) to a new band from San Francisco – Sly and the Family Stone. So Bob took off for France, and started a group in Paris called Head West. There were problems with management; in order to eat, Bob had to sell his last guitar. That's when Judy Wong called him.

Bob Welch flew to London with his last batch of francs. Mick picked him up at the Haslemere train station in his tiny Citroën Deux Chevaux, and took him out to Benifolds. They liked Bob's California vibes, Parisian flair, and soul-band roots. His rapport

Christine (Perfect) McVie in Chicken Shack days.

with the rest of the band was immediate, and they hired him to replace Jeremy without an audition.

Fleetwood Mac toured England in June after a month of rehearsals. It was the first time Bob Welch had performed two or three of his own songs before an audience, and everyone was relieved that Fleetwood Mac had a new sound. Their old blues audience was long gone; this was the era of the new glam-and-glitter bands – T Rex, Ziggy Stardust, and Spiders from Mars. Now bands wore make-up and minced around like pop tarts. Fleetwood Mac's flannel shirts and blue jeans were considered very passé.

The new edition of Fleetwood Mac, nevertheless, continued to find a receptive audience in America. Their new album, *Future Games*, was released in September 1971; its title track gained wide FM airplay. It was very satisfactory to everyone that Bob Welch had written and performed it in a breathy, Dylan-influenced talking style that managed to make an immediate connection to Fleetwood Mac's audience. An American tour that autumn was a box-office success. Fleetwood Mac headlined the Fillmore East (Van Morrison opened), broke attendance records in several cities, and added enough gigs for an additional two weeks. Fleetwood Mac was flying again. They had survived.

DISC
AND MUSIC ECHO 6p   USA 30c

SEPTEMBER 18, 1971

ROD STEWART IN CLOSE-UP

Lennon 'send-up' of Paul on LP
AND TROUBLE-HIT "IMAGINE" IS DELAYED—SEE P. 4

REFLECTING ON THE NEW FLEETWOOD MAC

Mick Fleetwood (right) talks about Mac's new writer (reflected in glasses).   see page three

Buffy — Judy for concerts

BUFFY ST MARIE and Judy Collins are coming to Britain for concert dates next month.

Buffy, in the chart with "Soldier Blue," returns for a solo London Royal Albert Hall booking on October 15; and agent Tony Burfield, of MAM, is arranging provincial appearances around October 27-31. She does Continental concerts also — in Stockholm (16), Copenhagen (18), Oslo (19) and Paris (23); returning to America on November 2.

JUDY COLLINS, meanwhile, comes in to play the Albert Hall on Tuesday, October 26 for promoter Robert Paterson. The "Amazing Grace" girl will stay in Britain about a week; and three or four provincial dates are also proposed before she moves to the Continent in the first week of November.

Cat Stevens
SONGS AND HANGUPS ON PAGE 7

EVERLY BROS.
THE DESTRUCTIVE MUSIC BUSINESS

Two hours after this picture was taken Jeremy Spencer disappeared

EXCLUSIVE STORY INSIDE

STONES IN FRANCE

JEREMY SPENCER, ex Fleetwood Mac guitarist, in a photograph by drummer Mick Fleetwood taken as the band's plane touched down in Los Angeles. Only two hours later Spencer disappeared off the streets of L.A.

CREEDENCE
break their silence

DEEP PURPLE

THE WHO

YES

Ringo has a go at John, Paul and George

The band spent most of 1972 touring in Europe and America. For months they worked second on a bill with Savoy Brown headlining and English blues shouter Long John Baldry opening. During a week off they recorded a new album, *Bare Trees*, at a studio in London. Hand-carrying the master tapes, they took off again for New York, where they were about to begin a summer tour opening for the then *au courant* metalateers, Deep Purple. To their horror, they discovered that American customs had x-rayed and damaged their master tapes. Harrowing all-night remixing sessions at Manhattan's Recording Plant ensued before the band could go out on the road.

Bare Trees was a good album, capturing the timelessness of Fleetwood Mac's country life and Chris's burgeoning songwriting ability. Her "Spare Me Little of Your Love" was an FM favorite, as was Bob's "Sentimental Lady." Everything seemed back on track, until Danny Kirwan went haywire.

He had been fragile to begin with, and the pressure of the departing of Peter Green and Jeremy Spencer had been building for some time. Introverted and eccentric, Danny was increasingly being shunned by the rest of the band until Mick, who had inherited the Green God's role of bandleader, was the only one speaking to him. Danny had taken Bob Welch's hiring badly, and the two guitar players were feuding.

In August 1972, at a college gig in
the Midwest, Danny went berserk
while the band was tuning up.
Because of an offhand remark,
Danny went into the bathroom and
smashed his head against the wall.
Bloody and raving, he then broke
his precious Les Paul guitar into
kindling. He refused to play;
instead he sat at the soundboard
and watched the band flounder as a
quartet. Afterwards, he critiqued
the show, noting to a stunned
Fleetwood that the tempo had
really been dragging during the
first few numbers.

Danny Kirwan was fired that
night and the band had to cancel
two weeks of gigs. Once again,
Fleetwood Mac limped home
to Hampshire in desperate need
of personnel.

Noting that young Americans
wished to boogie, management now
demanded the addition of a much-
dreaded "front man" – some
blustery belter who could rile up a
crowd: snakeskin boots and the old
fist in the air. So they raided Savoy
Brown for its singer, Dave Walker,
who really knew how to put a lot of
feeling into HOWYADOIN'
PITTSBURGH! Likewise, they
stole Long John Baldry's guitarist,
Bob Weston.

This six-piece Fleetwood Mac
played in Europe until December
1972, when they returned to
America to promote an album they
had quickly recorded at home
using the Rolling Stones' famous

Jeremy, my small friend took
flight one day never to return.

mobile studio. *Penguin* was named after John McVie's favorite bird, which in time became Fleetwood Mac's totemic trademark. Again the shows went well, but the band realized that Dave Walker wasn't really working out. He was an interpreter, and they needed an artist.

The band had to let him go after their return to England in early 1973, while they were working on their next album. Bob Welch had written some strong material for Walker, which had to be recast when Walker left. One song, inspired by the uncertainty of the group's checkered career, had been conceived as a showpiece for Walker's gutbucket approach. Freed of that burden, Bob drew upon his interest in psychic phenomena and, helped by Chris, came up with "Hypnotized," which became the standout track on *Mystery to Me*, Fleetwood Mac's strongest album since Peter Green had left.

The band went back to America in the fall of 1973 to earn its bread and butter. Earlier that year, Mike Vernon had rereleased "Albatross," which a new audience had sent into the Top Five. On the BBC, a *Top of the Pops* announcer informed a credulous Britain that Fleetwood Mac was no longer around, even though the band was touring

Mick, Bob, Danny, Chris & John

English universities at the time.

Fleetwood Mac had to play in the U.S., if only to remind themselves that they existed. But "Hypnotized" was already a hit when they arrived, and the band had an encouraging first month of playing colleges and dance halls. *Mystery to Me* was the first album in years that the group was incredibly proud of, and things looked pretty rosy until the group disintegrated in October, after Mick discovered that his wife was having an affair with his guitar player, Bob Weston.

Mick tried to maintain a stiff upper lip, but it proved impossible. After a gig in Nebraska, Bob Weston was sent home, and they canceled the rest of the make-or-break tour.

Mick was fried. He couldn't go on. Their manager was adamant. He warned them that he <u>owned</u> Fleetwood Mac. He also warned them that he refused to lose his reputation and business because of the whims of a bunch of irresponsible musicians. He warned them their careers would be over if they didn't do what he told them.

They hung up the phone, and Bob Welch said, "This guy thinks we're his slaves."

So Fleetwood Mac scattered to the winds, with plans to regroup as soon as possible. They were ill-prepared for what was about to happen to them.

Fleetwood Mac was hijacked in 1974 – perhaps the ultimate artistic nightmare any band ever had to endure. The story of the fake Fleetwood Mac stands as one of the most sordid and depraved episodes in the history of popular music. That the group managed to hang on, fight back, and eventually prevail is also one of the most inspiring sagas of the music business, still preserved in the oral tradition of rock musicians, wherever they may gather to hoist the one or two. The tale is a cautionary one for young apprentices who would follow the giants into battle, and underlines the notion that nothing normal ever happened to Fleetwood Mac.

After the *Mystery to Me* tour broke down, the bruised and battered musicians went their separate ways for a while. John McVie flew to Hawaii. Bob Welch and the band's gear went to Los Angeles along with John Courage, Fleetwood Mac's ever-faithful road manager. Christine McVie retreated to the security of Benifolds, while Mick Fleetwood lost himself in the game preserves of southern Africa until he and Jenny decided to get back together.

Management, meanwhile, ordered young Courage to meet Fleetwood Mac in New York with their gear. The tour was back on, he was told. Posters appeared for "The New Fleetwood Mac, Featuring Christine McVie and Mick Fleetwood." But when Courage landed, he realized that

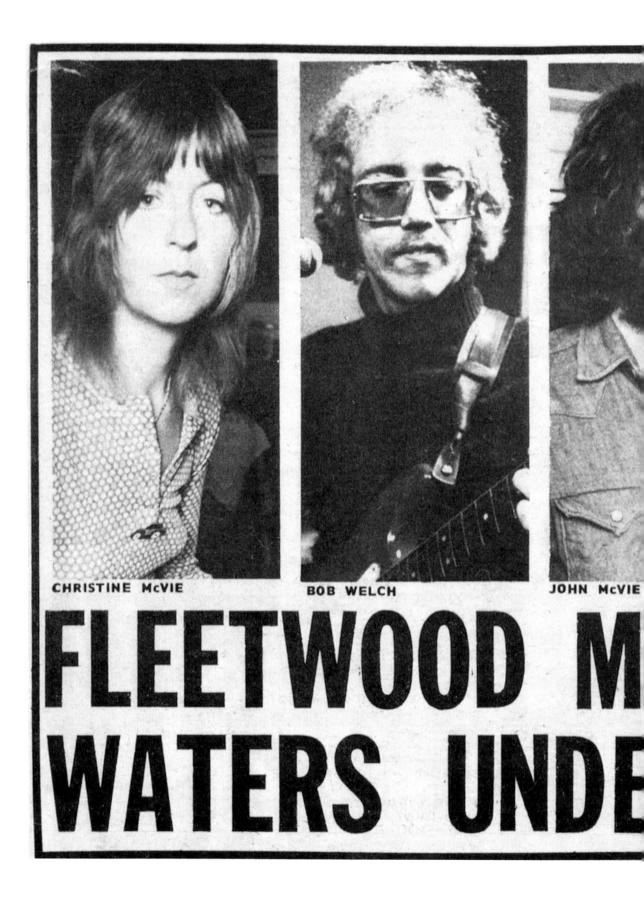

CHRISTINE McVIE   BOB WELCH   JOHN McVIE

FLEETWOOD M
WATERS UNDE

DANNY KIRWAN   MICK FLEETWOOD

AC—TROUBLED
R THE BRIDGE

management had hired a new set of musicians to <u>pose</u> as Fleetwood Mac. (They were actually musicians who had been working with Danny Kirwan, who had gone solo; they'd been told that Mick would be joining them after the first few dates.) Since he was in debt to Clifford Davis, Courage actually went on a few of Fake Mac's gigs. The audiences were confused at first when they didn't recognize anyone in the band; then they got angry. They threw bottles and garbage at the hapless musicians, who were either too stupid or too desperate to realize they were destroying the reputation of a band that had been slaving for six years.

The tour lasted only about ten days. John Courage skipped when he could stand no more, and called Bob Welch. By then, Mick was back in England, and soon the transatlantic phone lines were buzzing. They quickly learned that their manager had them in a contractual headlock. They were unable to record as Fleetwood Mac, unable to tour. Court injunctions had been obtained against them, and their concert fees and royalties were frozen. No money was coming in. Mick hired lawyers, who showed him contracts they'd signed as drunken teenagers, years before. It looked as if they didn't even own their name. When the press got hold of the story in February

1974, it sunk whatever credibility Fleetwood Mac had left. It seemed like the end of the road.

It was Mick Fleetwood who realized that Fleetwood Mac had to get out of England as soon as possible. Bob Welch was urging him to bring the band to California. Mick was keen, and so was John, but Christine McVie's life was tied up in the home they'd all been working for, and she was reluctant to leave her family, pull up stakes, and migrate to Los Angeles. Mick begged her to try it for six months, and if she didn't like it they'd all come home. So Fleetwood Mac left England in the spring of 1974, and never looked back.

The band arrived at LAX with $7,200, no manager, no equipment, no staff, no credibility, and a record contract that could be best described as tenuous. They settled into rented quarters in Laurel Canyon and Malibu and started to rebuild their lives. Mick Fleetwood assumed the band's managerial duties. After what they'd been through, no one in the band wanted another manager. Then they faced the task of introducing themselves to

1973 Christine, Dave Walker, Bob, Mick, Bob Weston & John & Mick's dog Bailey.

(Far left) Band rehearsals at Benifolds.

57

their own record company, who knew they were in litigation in England and might not even own their name and the Fleetwood Mac trademark.

So Mick Fleetwood began to go to meetings in Hollywood. He discovered that the one thing Fleetwood Mac had going for it was their audience – loyal, consistent, and ever faithful, ever sure. The record company knew the band produced good records on schedule that consistently sold 300,000 copies to the same people. The scenario rarely varied: no hit singles, the band fell apart on tour, and came back a year or so later with another record. The joke was that Fleetwood Mac paid Warner Brothers' light bill.

Although they weren't used to negotiating directly with the musicians whose records they sold, Warner Brothers decided to give the band a chance to record in America after Bill Graham personally stuck up for them with testimonial letters and promises of bookings. So, in June 1974, they began work on a new album, *Heroes Are Hard to Find*, the first

"Dave Walker and Bob Weston were, if but briefly, to make their mark on Fleetwood Mac during the band's tumultuous times." - M.F.
(Far left above) Dave Walker
(Far left middle) Bob Weston
(Far left below) Christine

Fleetwood Mac album recorded entirely in America. Predictably, Clifford Davis tried to prevent its release in September, but American courts allowed Fleetwood Mac to proceed. They spent that autumn touring the U.S. on a crusade to repair their tattered image. They'd once been headliners working for five grand a night. Now they were opening shows for $1,500 a shot, often returning money to promoters after the show didn't draw a big crowd. Past burn-outs and canceled shows had hurt the band with the industry people – booking agents, concert promoters, radio stations – they needed to survive. So on they slogged, mending fences, greeting their still-loyal audience, playing for time.

After forty-three shows, Bob Welch had had enough. The strain of the road and reconstructing Fleetwood Mac had drained his energy, and he decided to withdraw after the tour. So Chris, John, and Mick once again began to try to find some new heroes to keep Fleetwood Mac on the air. Mick told the McVies not to worry, that he was sure somebody good would turn up.

Bob Welch

(Far right) Fleetwood Mac in Los Angeles, October 1974, prior to Bob Welch's departure.

FLEETWOOD MAC · FLEETWOOD MAC

<u>Ah</u> !! That feeling again . . .
Magic.

The undeniable sensation of rightness
that came from moment one ~~when~~
Stevie and Lindsey became part of
Fleetwood Mac. It was as if Merlin himself
could not have ~~conceived~~ concocted
a spell more perfect. A spell that was
not only to last well over a decade,
but would lead Christine, Stevie,
Lindsey, John and myself on a personal
and most certainly Musical odyssey
that I think for all of us has to be
a moment in time that will
always be part of us.

Mick was confident because he had already seen the future, even if he didn't quite know it yet. During a break in the *Heroes Are Hard to Find* tour, he had started to look for a studio in which to record the next album. He was just doing his managerial thing. While shopping for groceries, he ran into an acquaintance named Thomas Christian, who told Mick about a good studio called Sound City among the tracts of the San Fernando Valley. So Mick piled his two daughters and the groceries into the back of his seedy old Cadillac and went over to inspect the studio.

The place was owned by an engineer named Keith Olsen. To demonstrate the sound of the studio, he played "Frozen Love," a track that had been recorded there by an obscure duo. Mick loved the great guitar playing on the track, and liked the sound of the room as well, but his attention had been caught by what he saw on the other side of the glass in the next studio. It was a young woman with honey-colored hair, extremely attractive, wearing a skirt and an Indian print cotton shirt. She was working on a vocal track. Mick turned to the engineer and asked,

Fleetwood Mac at Beachwood Stables , Hollywood 1975.

64

"Who's that pretty girl in there?"

Someone said her name:

Stevie Nicks.

Then the guitar player on "Frozen Love," who was also working elsewhere in the studio, came in to be introduced to Mick:

Lindsey Buckingham.

Fleetwood said thank you very much and went back out on the road. When Bob Welch quit in late December 1974, Fleetwood called Sound City and told them he wanted that guitar player he'd heard – "Buckingham, was it?" – to be in Fleetwood Mac. Mick was told that Lindsey and his girlfriend were a team, and that they didn't think Lindsey would join without Stevie.

"Right," Fleetwood said. "We'll take 'em both!"

Who were the new members of Fleetwood Mac? Two starving young musicians who, Stevie would later declare, "fell into the American dream."

Her musical career began when she was a little girl in Arizona. Her grandfather, A.J. Nicks, was a country-style musician who used to take her along when he played in saloons. Stevie would dance on the bar, and the customers loved it. But

The band at the S.I.R. Studio lot behind Penguin Promotions Office 1976.

65

Stevie was only five, and the parents refused to allow the old man to take his granddaughter on the road with him, causing a rift in the family that took some time to heal.

Stevie's father was an executive who moved his family quite a bit as he changed jobs. She started high school in L.A., where she had her first little group, the Change In Times, named after the Bob Dylan song. The family moved to the Bay area, where Stevie attended college and began to work on the fringes of the San Francisco music scene. Her group, Fritz, was a late sixties opening act for the likes of Jefferson Airplane, Big Brother & the Holding Company, and Moby Grape. The boys in Fritz had a policy toward their girl singer: Hands off Stevie Nicks. She took this as professional jealousy, because she was the focal point of the band and got all the attention, but the bass player, Lindsey Buckingham, knew better. He was from an athletic California family. His father owned a coffee company, and Lindsey grew up listening to Buddy Holly, the Everly Brothers, the Kingston Trio, and especially Brian Wilson's Beach

Christine, Lindsey and Stevie

(Far right) "Ahh... very nice cloth." – M.F.

Boys. Lindsey and Stevie knew each other slightly in high school, an acquaintance that was renewed when they both found themselves in Fritz. But the band was unable to break out of opener status, and broke up in 1971. Stevie and Lindsey stayed together to write songs, and also became lovers. They had supreme confidence in their music, and migrated to Los Angeles in search of a breakthrough. Working as Buckingham Nicks, they recorded an album at Sound City. When this record flopped, they continued to write new songs – one was called "Rhiannon" – in hopes of getting another record deal. To put bread on the table, Lindsey went on the road with Don Everly's band; Stevie cleaned houses and worked as a waitress at a Bob's Big Boy. On New Year's Eve, this struggling couple were wondering if 1975 was going to turn out a little better for them, when Olsen walked in the room and told them the Mick Fleetwood wanted them for his band.

Fleetwood Mac met Buckingham Nicks for dinner at a Mexican restaurant. Stevie arrived first, still wearing a flapper's outfit from her

"Spring Break" Austin, Texas 1976

waitressing job at a roaring-twenties theme cafe. Years later, she would recall, "I watched Fleetwood Mac drive up in these two clunky old Cadillacs with big tail fins, and I was in awe."

The five musicians settled at a table and ordered margaritas. That was it. The crucial vote, as always, was Christine's; only she could decide whether she could work with another woman in the band. Chemistry was essential, or it couldn't happen. After it was clear that the two ladies were getting along – Chris slipped Mick a wink and a nod – Fleetwood leaned over to Stevie and Lindsey and said, "Want to join?"

They both said yes. Lindsey asked if they wanted them to audition. Mick told them that they hired musicians on instinct, and had never even held a successful audition.

Thus Fleetwood Mac was reborn as an Anglo-Californian band in January 1975.

The band put Lindsey and Stevie on salary – $200 per week each – and paid off some of their back rent as well. Chris went back to England to see her family

(Above) Mick and Lindsey
(Below left) Greg Thomason and Richard Dashut
(Below right) Christine and Lindsey
(Far left) On the road. Mick, his wife Jenny and daughters Amy Rose and Lucy.

while John, Mick, and Lindsey began rehearsing in a garage on Pico Boulevard. There was an instant sonic rapport between Lindsey and his new rhythm section, and they hadn't even heard the three voices yet. This happened when the whole band convened in their booking agency's basement and began to rehearse Chris's new song "Say That You Love Me." Chris remembered, "We were playing this song and I heard this incredible sound – our three voices – and I said to myself, 'Is this me singing?' I couldn't believe how exciting it sounded that first time."

Mick Fleetwood booked studio time for his new band in February 1975, but before the sessions began, Buckingham Nicks played a farewell show in Birmingham, Alabama, where their album had enjoyed a freak local success. After the show, Lindsey told the sold-out audience that they were joining Fleetwood Mac. Any doubts on Fleetwood Mac's new lineup were dispelled when the three songwriters exchanged demo tapes. Mick Fleetwood was astonished when he heard Chris's demos and Stevie's, both containing songs that would become standards, on the same day. Chris had, "Over My Head," "Warm Ways," and

"Sugar Daddy." Stevie contributed "Landslide" and "Rhiannon." Lindsey brought in "Monday Morning" and "So Afraid." Stevie's "Crystal" from *Buckingham Nicks* was recast as a Fleetwood Mac song as well. The sessions at Sound City also produced "Blue Letter," written by the country-rock Curtis Brothers, who were using the studio at the same time; and the group collaboration, "World Turning." By June 1975 the album was finished, and Mick Fleetwood – rock soldier, ardent gigster – was frothing at the mouth to get the band on the road and show off their new look.

Some instinct had Mick convinced; the new band was gonna be *massive*.

First Fleetwood had to sell the band to his record company. He played the new album, *Fleetwood Mac*, for Warner executives, who said: Hey, this is great! Maybe it'll sell three hundred and <u>fifty</u> thousand! But Mick wasn't content with being the act that paid the label's electric bill. He was convinced they were going to sell <u>tonnage</u> of this new music. Mick met with label chief Mo Ostin, and laid it

Miami, Florida 1976
"As my father, Wing Commander Fleetwood once said- 'Let's face it Mick, penguins just weren't meant to fly.'" -M.F.

74

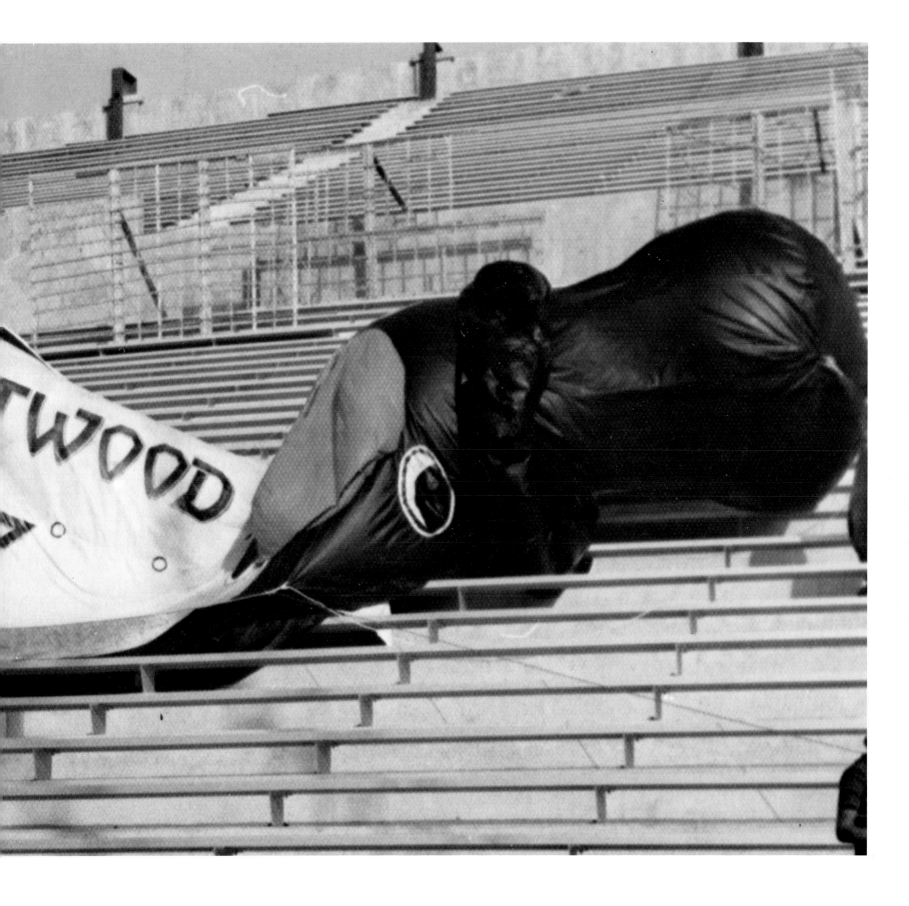

THIS WEEK	LAST WEEK	Weeks on C	ART Tit Lal
⭐ 1		1	40	FLE Ru War
⭐ 2		2	10	LI Si

ST

el, Number (Dist. Label)

TWOOD MAC

ours
er Bros. BSK 3010

DA RONSTADT

iple Dreams

SF 104

on the line: We're on to something here. It's going to be _very_ big. Believe in us, or let us go.

Mick wanted to get out and play even before the album was released. The label pointed out that Fleetwood Mac broke up every time it toured. Mick assured them it wouldn't happen this time. So the band made its world debut on May 15, 1975, in El Paso, Texas.

Fleetwood Mac's show in those days began without Stevie Nicks. The band, fronted by Chris, would run through some of their familiar hits, with Lindsey firing away on rock & roll guitar. Stevie gradually emerged singing in the vocal mix, and then completely took over the show when it was "Rhiannon" time. As Lindsey picked those legendary chords and the band began to smoke, Stevie would step up to the microphone and tell the audience, "This is a song about a Welsh witch." She performed this intense homage to the ancient Celtic goddess wearing a black chiffon cape that fluttered like diaphanous wings as she danced.

The climax of the song was a catharsis of her wailing verses and Lindsey's furiously piercing electric guitar. No one who saw

Oakland, California 1977

A day on the Green— "There we were, literally standing in a pot of gold." -M.F.

these early performances ever forgot them. Stevie Nicks, singing like the angel of the rodeo and moving around the stage like a dream, was pure magic.

During the summer of 1975, Fleetwood Mac opened for Loggins & Messina and the Guess Who. When they headlined midsized theaters and didn't sell out, Mick and John Courage would give money back to the promoters to ensure future loyalty when the band was really about to break open. The first single was "Over My Head," remixed for AM radio by a producer who had worked with the Jackson 5. As it began to climb the charts, Fleetwood Mac stayed on the road. They played ninety shows during the last four months of the year, driving around America in two rented station wagons. Chris, John and Mick were old hands at this brutal pace. It was trial-by-fire for Lindsey, who became an incredibly fluid rock guitarist amid the din of battle. But it almost killed Stevie Nicks. As "Rhiannon" got more and more brilliant and developed ever greater emotion, the song began

A Day on the Green– "Another day, another gig. Great times to remember– we were flying high. Indeed most, if not all of our performances were to over sixty thousand fans. If you like... a dream come true." -M.F.

to shred Stevie's voice. She danced so much that she was exhausted afterwards. Yet every night she and Chris would have to get back into the car and drive to the next gig, with amplifiers for pillows. Bad food, no sleep, and illness taxed Stevie's frail constitution, and her bandmates became alarmed at her thinness.

She also suffered the barbs of critics, who didn't understand the new sense of rock theater she was trying to convey. Their negative comments hurt Stevie terribly, and she briefly thought about quitting. No dynamic woman had fronted a major rock band since Janis Joplin had died four years earlier, and it took the press some time to get used to Stevie's strong yet ultrafeminine presence. But Fleetwood Mac's fans, old and new, understood the new band perfectly. Chris's glorious, womanly singing propelled "Over My Head" into the U.S. Top Ten in November 1975. Everyone who was around then knew this was a new kind of music. Women were back in the rock & roll arena as equals for the first time in years, and FM radio loved it. (For the rest of the decade, FM practically stood for Fleetwood Mac in America.) By Christmas, *Fleetwood Mac* had sold a million-and-a-half records. Mick's instincts had been dead on. And the musicians <u>knew</u> they were on

(Far right, left photo) "Bill—We must stop meeting like this!" -M.F.

the cusp of some immense artistic breakthrough as well. All the musicians knew by early 1976 that the emotional weather of the group was going to be very stormy. Christine McVie had stopped sharing hotel rooms with husband John while they were still on tour. Lindsey and Stevie's seven-year relationship ended when Stevie walked out. Likewise, Jenny Boyd Fleetwood took her two daughters and fled the California fast land for the relative sanity of England, ending her and Mick's marriage as well. These were the conditions under which Fleetwood Mac was forced to record its new music. There was never any question of breaking up the band after all they'd been through. But, with their ex-spouses in the band, there was literally no place to hide. The new love songs the group was preparing were like raw wounds,

"John is a man who likes two ladies in his life. He's wise, he always makes sure one of them is a boat." -M.F.

(Above) The *Challenge*

(Below) Mick and John in St. Thomas, Virgin Islands.

(Far right) John aboard his first boat *Adelie* at Marina Del Rey, Los Angeles.

(Previous Page) "Christine and Bob Welch at a party, 1977". – M.F.

and everyone made tremendous emotional sacrifices just to show up at the studio.

The album was recorded at The Record Plant, in bohemian Sausalito, California, where Mick had felt the vibes would be mellow. Instead, they were horrendous. First, the house engineer was dropped, replaced by Richard Dashut, a longtime colleague, and his associate Ken Caillat, who would coproduce. Then things started to go wrong. A piano took four days to tune. A tape machine they called jaws began to destroy finished tapes. As word spread around the Bay area that glamorous Fleetwood Mac was recording, the studio's lounges began to fill up with strangers tapping razors on mirrors. It was like a constant cocktail party, with the actual musicians barely speaking to each other.

And yet...the music was transporting. "Go Your Own Way" was a killer. Stevie and Lindsey sang "I Don't Want to Know" as if for their very lives. Chris's "Don't Stop" mingled heartbreak, disappointment, and hope for a healing future. "The

1978 Fleetwood Mac Halloween party at Lindsey's house.

(Far left) Coneheads

Chain" existed only as a batch of disembodied riffs; when they were finally assembled later in the year in Los Angeles with new lyrics by Stevie Nicks, they embodied Fleetwood Mac's new romantic line-up.

While all this was going on, "Rhiannon" was released as a single, went straight to the top of the charts, and established Fleetwood Mac as a superstar band. Their label pressed them for the new album, and were repeatedly told by Mick Fleetwood that it wasn't ready. Unsatisfied with their work, and obsessed with perfection, the band even canceled a lucrative spring tour so the album, whose working title was *Yesterday's Gone*, could be remixed.

When Fleetwood Mac finally did tour during the summer of 1976, it was a different world. Playing stadiums in tandem with their friendly rivals, the Eagles, Fleetwood Mac would look out from the stage and see a new generation of fans: thousands of young girls in black top hats and lots of chiffon – Stevie's stage costume. When Stevie came out and announced, "This is a song about a Welsh witch," these ladies went mad with delight, like a human sea of swaying lace.

Stevie in her ballet studio at home, 1979.

(Far right) Stevie practices ballet on the road.

Still, the new album would not quite jell. But on September 4, 1976, *Fleetwood Mac* replaced *Frampton Comes Alive* as the number one album on the *Billboard* chart, after an astonishing fifty-six-week march.

Under the firm guidance of Seedy Management, Mick and John's corporate identity, the Fleetwood Mac team continued to craft their new album. The louder the record company screamed for new product, the more Mick advised them to be patient. Art took longer than product. Meanwhile, the band continued its glamorous rise, appearing on magazine covers and as winners on nationally televised awards shows, mobbed by their adoring fans at every public appearance. The band appreciated the humor, irony, and the pitfalls that sudden success had to offer. The supersensitive Stevie Nicks found her sudden stardom tinged with occasional regret. Riding

Tusk Tour 1980

(Above) John, Christine and Lindsey

(Below) Robin Anderson, Christie Alsbury, Stevie and Dwayne Taylor

(Far left) Mick Fleetwood and Penguin Promotions office manager Judy Wong taking care of business. "Back in those days we managed ourselves. No wonder I lost most of my hair!" - M.F.

alone in a limo after a post-concert encounter with ardent fans who had pressed flowers, silver, and turquoises into her hands, Stevie said that now she knew how Marilyn Monroe must have felt.

Some of the ironies were murderous. During that autumn of 1976, Fleetwood Mac returned to England for a round of press interviews. As they entered their London hotel, they were met by a portly, aging hippie whose ghetto blaster boomed out bad disco music. It was Peter Green. Seeing their old Green God in such poor mental health deeply shocked Mick, John, and Chris, reminding them of the transitory nature of success.

An even ruder awakening met them when their jet touched down at LAX. The English members of the band had entered the U.S. on tourist visas almost two years earlier, and now the authorities didn't want to let them back in. Disaster was averted when the dreaded "green cards" were quickly procured. One byproduct of this encounter with immigration authorities was Mick's remarriage to Jenny in order to regularize his family's presence in California.

By the end of 1976, the new album was being sequenced. The final running order was "Second Hand News" (Lindsey), "Dreams" (Stevie), "Never Going Back

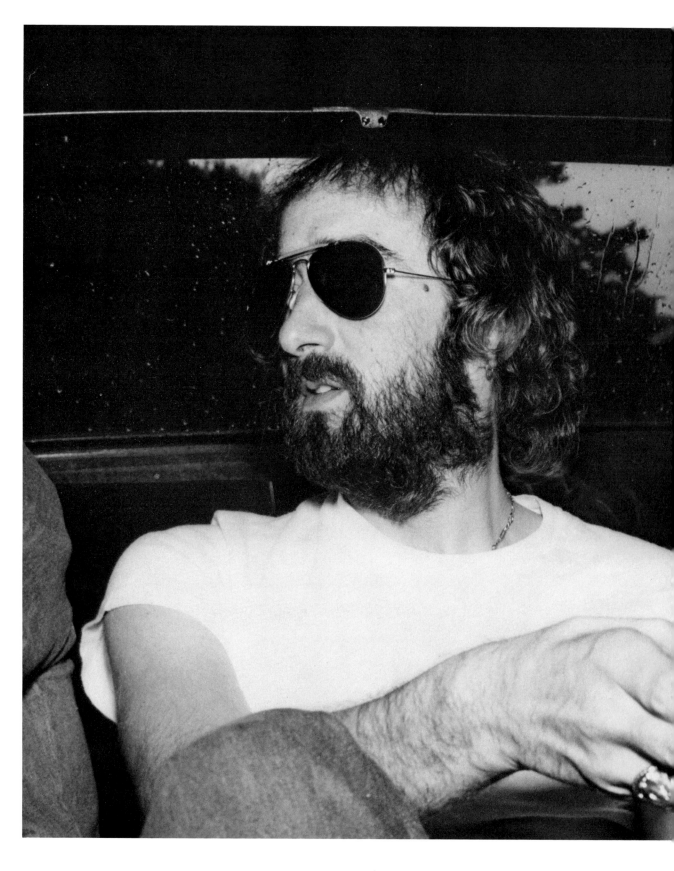

Again" (Lindsey), "Don't Stop" (Chris), and "Go Your Own Way" (Lindsey). Chris's "Songbird" closed out side one. "The Chain" (credited to the group: Stevie wrote the lyrics) opened the second side followed by "You Make Loving Fun" (Christine), "I Don't Want to Know" (Stevie), "Oh Daddy" (Christ), and Stevie's "Gold Dust Woman." In addition, Stevie Nicks' extraordinary "Silver Springs" from these sessions appeared as the B-side of "Go Your Own Way" when it was released as a single.

The band was listening to the final mix-down of the final sequence in the studio when Chris asked how they were going to title the album. John McVie remembered that the songs all sounded to him like a bunch of rumours. And indeed, Fleetwood Mac's romantic tornado of the past year had spun off many little cyclones of gossip about who was doing what to whom. Fleetwood Mac's adventures were the hottest dish of the day in southern California, and it seemed only reasonable to release their new music under the title *Rumours* in February 1977.

"Go Your Own Way" was an immediate hit single. FM radio put it into play and once again Fleetwood Mac was all over the road. *Rumours* shipped 800,000 units, a milestone for their label. Soon it would make history.

The band went back on the
road that spring, playing the round
of bowls, domes, arenas, gardens,
and coliseums. Top-hatted Stevie
Nicks was in heaven, the crown
princess of pop music.
"Rhiannon" continued as a show-
stopping centerpiece, but it took a
toll on her voice, which was
treated and ministered to with
every therapy known. Stevie's
instrument changed on that tour, a
sacrifice she made for her muse.
When they returned to
England in April, playing old
haunts for the first time in years,
they learned that the Green God
was in a mental hospital, having
narrowly avoided prison after
threatening his accountant and
demanding that his royalty
payments be *stopped*.
The band stayed on the road
for much of 1977. *Rumours* topped
the album charts beginning in
May. There would not be another
number-one record that year, as
Rumours stayed at number one for
thirty-one consecutive weeks.
And the hits kept on coming:
"Don't Stop" spent the summer
on the singles charts; the brilliant
"You Make Loving Fun" dominated
the airwaves that autumn.
Fleetwood Mac finished the
year with a triumphal march along
the Pacific Rim: Japan, Australia,
New Zealand, and Hawaii. By
the beginning of

Stevie Nicks

1978, sales of *Rumours* were almost incomprehensible: 8 million sold, 800,000 more selling every week, still number one in the U.S. and double platinum in England, with international name recognition unheard of since the end of the Beatles. (With total sales to date exceeding well over 20 million copies, *Rumours* has become the most successful recording ever made by a rock group and stands as one of the best-selling albums in history, its sales record broken only by Michael Jackson's *Thriller* and two disco-era movie soundtracks.)

That year's award shows seemed like mere formalities to the coronation of Fleetwood Mac: a clean sweep of the American Music Awards, the Grammy for Best Album, four *Rolling Stone* readers' poll victories. And all this success was contagious. Guided by the often inscrutable Seedy Management, Bob Welch came back into the fold. His great *French Kiss* solo album and "Ebony Eyes" single were among the major records of 1978.

Fleetwood Mac, reigning monarchs of rock, now spent the next eighteen months readjusting their lives and working on new

Lindsey at home in his artificial rain room.

songs. The musical climate of the late 1970s had been fragmented by the cultural shock wave of the punk movement a year or two earlier. These were the days of brash young New Wave bands; but Fleetwood Mac, in the person of its resident wizard Lindsey Buckingham, was not about to trot along to Boring Old Fartdom, which is where blowhards like the Clash were trying to send them, along with Elton John, the Stones, and Led Zeppelin.

Not that Lindsey needed much prodding. He was totally committed to his art, to the exclusion of almost everything else, and felt the formulaic duplication of the megasuccessful whoosh of *Rumours* would have meant a betrayal of artistic standards. While Stevie and Chris crafted their songs in the million-dollar studio designed specifically for Fleetwood Mac at a Los Angeles

Recording of the U.S.C Trojan marching band at Dodger Stadium for the "Tusk" track, 1979. "'What we need on this track is a big band,' I said, referring to Lindsey's song 'Tusk.' My God—I don't think a band could get much bigger! John missed that day, so there he is—larger than life, right behind me cut out of cardboard." - M.F.

(Previous page) Dodger Stadium, Los Angeles 1979

complex called The Village Recorder, Lindsey preferred to develop his material at his home studio, where his fierce powers of concentration would be undisturbed.

Fleetwood Mac was at the apogee of its flight during its *Penguin Country Summer Safari* tour that roamed American stadia in July 1978. Performing with a pagan streak of green tinting her long hair, Stevie was the Compleat Enchantress, learning to hold immense crowds in the palm of her hand as she intoned the verses of her songs. Meanwhile, she and Mick had a brief affair, and Chris had taken up with the wild, doomed Beach Boy Dennis Wilson, who remained a close friend of the band until his drowning some years later. And Peter Green resurfaced in Los Angeles, seemingly healthy, even playing the guitar again. Mick negotiated a lucrative record deal for the Green God, who refused to sign the contract at the last minute, when his old demons returned to haunt him.

By the summer of 1979, Fleetwood Mac had twenty new songs ready to release, and not one seemed unworthy. The range of the double album they proposed was staggering. The music was innovative,

These pages are devoted to Richard Dashut and Ken Caillat who were so much part of the recording process that while in the studio it was like having a sixth and seventh member in the band I haven't worked with a better team before or since Two greater friends Fleetwood Mac never had

sometimes eccentric or self-indulgent, even borderline weird. The title track to the album that would be called *Tusk* was recorded in an empty Dodger Stadium with 112 members of the University of Southern California Trojan Marching Band in an attempt to replicate the feeling of a village brass band that Mick had encountered on a hung-over morning during a visit to Normandy.

Other tracks sounded more like Fleetwood Mac. "Sara" was one of Stevie Nicks' major works, and "Sisters of the Moon" became an anthem for her fans. Chris's "Brown Eyes" and "Never Make Me Cry" were among her best, most emotional love songs.

Part of the legend that has grown around *Tusk* is the story that Warner Brothers executives, rabid for the sequel to *Rumours*, listened to the quirky new album and had a group vision of their Christmas bonuses flying out the window. Not only did no blockbuster single stare them in the face, but they also arranged a promotional stunt that notoriously misfired when the

Christine McVie at the Village Recording Studio, West Los Angeles.

entire album was played over Westwood One, the country's major FM radio network, allowing fans to tape the whole work in sequence, completely avoiding *Tusk*'s unprecedented sixteen dollar price tag. The recession and the backlash that gripped the music business in 1979 had even reached Big Mac, as it was usually called in the press. Fleetwood Mac realized that they would now have to expend enormous energy to promote their new music and compete with the impossibly successful legacy of their recent past. Little did anyone realize that this effort would nearly kill the band for good.

Fleetwood Mac embarked on a year-long crusade to sell their new album in October 1979. At the time, the *Tusk* tour was one of the largest rock spectacles ever assembled, perhaps the supreme challenge to a great rock band that had nonetheless been off the road for more than a year by then. But after a few spotty shows, Fleetwood Mac hit what must have been its prime, playing some of the most inspired and bewitching shows of their lives.

Tusk tour 1980

Madison Square Gardens, New York,

(Far left) Lindsey Buckingham

The *Tusk*-era Fleetwood Mac
were a disparate bunch. Standing
backstage early on, Stevie
checked out the motley styles of
her colleagues and remarked
that everyone looked like they
were going to a different place.
John McVie might be wearing
bits of Dodger uniforms.
Lindsey had shed his curly long
hair for a short New Wave do
and a well-cut gray suit. Chris
wore a sophisticated Bel Air
look, while Mick – heavily
bearded, hatted, and gruff –
sported his usual breeches,
stockings, and pub toilet balls
suspended from his belt. As the
focal point of the shows, Stevie
went through six costume
changes, attended by a wardrobe
mistress, hair stylists and
makeup girl. It was a far cry
from the bone-jarring austerity
of the early days. Now the band
traveled in its own chartered jet.
Six limos waited at the foot of
the ramp at every stop. The
most expensive hotel suites in
the world were redecorated and
supplied with grand pianos. The
whole trip was fueled by
mountains of cocaine. This tour
was how Fleetwood Mac
acquired its richly deserved

"I think I look very comfortable sitting on the
hard end of the table. In fact I was to vacate that
end of the table for many years to come!" - M.F.
(Previous page) Tusk tour rehearsal 1979.

City of Los Angeles

PROCLAMATION

Fleetwood Mac
DAY

WHEREAS, FLEETWOOD MAC, THE INTERNATIONALLY-KNOWN WARNER BROS. RECORDS RECORDING GROUP, HAS SOLD MORE THAN 20 MILLION RECORDS AND HAS PLAYED LIVE BEFORE MORE THAN TWO MILLION PEOPLE IN TEN COUNTRIES AROUND THE WORLD SINCE 1975; AND

WHEREAS, ON OCTOBER 12, 1979, THEIR LONG-AWAITED NEW ALBUM, "TUSK," WILL BE RELEASED, FOLLOWED BY A LENGTHY WORLD TOUR THAT WILL CONTINUE WELL INTO 1980. THEIR LAST ALBUM, "RUMOURS" HAS SOLD MORE THAN 13 MILLLION COPIES WORLDWIDE; AND

WHEREAS, THE MEMBERS OF FLEETWOOD MAC TAKE TIME TO SUPPORT THE CAUSES THAT CONCERN THEM, IN 1977, A BENEFIT CONCERT APPEARANCE IN BERKELEY, CALIFORNIA RAISED MORE THAN $30,000 FOR THE JACQUES COUSTEAU SOCIETY AND ITS ECOLOGY CAMPAIGNS. WHILE A SHOW IN TUCSON STADIUM, STILL ONE OF THE LARGEST GATHERINGS EVER IN THE STATE OF ARIZONA, RAISED UPWARDS OF $300,000 FOR THE AMERICAN HEART ASSOCIATION. THE PUBLISHING ROYALTIES TO ONE OF THE SONGS ON THE FORTHCOMING "TUSK" ALBUM HAS BEEN ASSIGNED TO THE "MUSIC FOR UNICEF" CAMPAIGN AND WILL REPRESENT A CONSIDERABLE DONATION TO UNICEF; AND

WHEREAS, ON OCTOBER 10, 1979, FLEETWOOD MAC — MICK FLEETWOOD, CHRISTINE MC VIE, LINDSEY BUCKINGHAM, STEVIE NICKS, AND JOHN MC VIE — WILL BE HONORED WITH THE PRESENTATION OF A STAR ON HOLLYWOOD BOULEVARD'S WALK OF FAME:

NOW, THEREFORE, I, TOM BRADLEY, MAYOR OF THE CITY OF LOS ANGELES, DO HEREBY PROCLAIM OCTOBER 10, 1979 AS "FLEETWOOD MAC DAY" IN LOS ANGELES IN RECOGNITION OF FLEETWOOD MAC'S OUTSTANDING CONTRIBUTIONS TO THE FIELD OF MUSIC AND ENTERTAINMENT, AND FOR THEIR HUMANITARIAN EFFORTS IN SUPPORTING OUR WORTHY CHARITIES.

OCTOBER 10, 1979

Tom Bradley
MAYOR

reputation for traveling <u>de luxe</u>.

One of the early shows, in St. Louis, was filmed by Warner Brothers. Let's stop the tape during the climax of "Sara." Stevie Nicks is completely wrapped in a long crimson shawl, standing alone and bent back from the mike, her hair a tawny mass of ringlets. The spotlight gives the red figure a surreal glow, an image of great pre-Raphaelite beauty, like a painting by Burne-Jones. Push

---

1980 Hawaii. Richard Dashut's going away party.

"All work and no play makes Jack a dull boy." - M.F.

(Far left above) Dennis Dunstan, Mick's personal bodyguard from 1979 to 1987, now Mick's manager.

"Dennis literally walked into my life at the beginning of the 'Tusk' tour. From that moment on he has stood by me through thick and thin. I thank him." - M.F.

(Far left below) Mick at home in Beverly Hills with his wife Sara, daughters Lucy, Amy and mother Biddy.

(Far left above right) Fleetwood Mac backstage at Madison Square Garden with publicist Sharon Weisz and tour manager John Courage.

(Far left bottom right) John Courage, Fleetwood Mac's road manager from 1972 to present.

"John Courage, better known to us all as Colonel Courage, would often go above and beyond his duty to protect and guide Fleetwood Mac from one corner of the world to the other."

(Page 111) Hollywood 1979

"As I often wondered and as Stevie says– What does happen 'after the glitter fades'?" - M.F.

"play" again and Lindsey's custom guitar is running circles around the song, while the rhythm rocks steady and Stevie stands back and delivers the final prayer – "All I ever wanted…" – while the fans pour waves and waves of ovation and adulation. There was something almost religious about the fervor.

The band capped the first leg of the tour that December with five sold-out nights at the Forum in L.A. and three at San Francisco's Cow Palace. During a press conference at their hotel, the band was asked when they were breaking up. Mick acknowledged that some of them were indeed contemplating solo projects, but maintained that despite persistent rumors the band would not break up. Then Mick went into a hypoglycemic seizure. Christine applied her healing touch in front of uncomprehending scribes, and the press conference continued.

The Cow Palace shows were the last of the 1970s. For Fleetwood Mac, it had been a hell of a decade.

"After the gig" – M.F.

(Far left) "During the gig"

(Page 118) Special limited edition Tusk promotional poster of photographer Peter Beard's private journals.

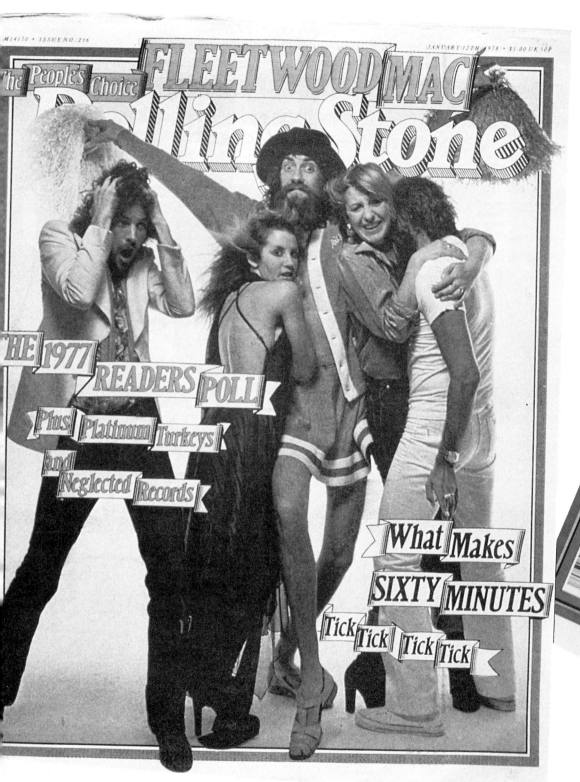

M14170 · ISSUE NO. 256

The People's Choice

FLEETWOOD MAC

Rolling Stone

JANUARY 12TH 1978 · $1.00 UK 50P

THE 1977 READERS POLL

Plus Platinum Turkeys and Neglected Records

What Makes SIXTY MINUTES Tick Tick Tick Tick

Readers' and Critics' Awards

THE POLICE
Best New Band

DUSTIN HOFFMAN
Back on Top in 'Kramer vs. Kramer'

America's OLYMPIC HOPEFULS

1980 Guide to Musical Instruments

FLEE
They

MARCH 24th, 1977 • ISSUE NO. 235

SM14170

ROLLING STONE

WOMEN IN EROTIC LITERATURE
By Francine du Plessix Gray

FLEETWOOD MAC

TRUE LIFE CONFESSIONS

By Cameron Crowe
with Photographs by
Annie Leibovitz

(adjacent magazine cover, partially visible)

STONE

WOOD MAC

...red to Be Different!

Last gig of the Tusk tour at the Hollywood Bowl.

TANGO

After the making of "Tusk," and a seemingly endless year of touring which finished at the Hollywood Bowl, we were left with ~~the~~ a sensation that the roller-coaster ride might very well have come to a permanent end.

As ~~things~~ turned out, the working formula ~~of the~~ band became much more complicated. If you like, more like a chess game that to this day is still being played out move by move.

With Lindsey's departure after the making of "Tango"—Billy Burnette and Rick Vito joined Fleetwood Mac, yet again adding new pieces to the board.

"Yes this long dance seems
to find new steps to dance by"
Mick

Thank God for Africa you have always been there for me. I don't think a drummer boy often gets this happy

Early 1980. Ted Kennedy was trying to unseat Jimmy Carter. The Soviets were moving deeper into Afghanistan. Ronald Reagan wanted to be president. Stevie Nicks moved into a little beach house and began working on her first solo album. The Fleetwood Mac flew to Japan for a series of rabidly anticipated shows. In Tokyo, Paul McCartney had just spent two weeks in jail for trying to smuggle some reefer, and before the *Tusk* tour could play the Land of the Rising Sun, Fleetwood Mac had to hold a press conference to publicly deny using marijuana. (A certain guitar player might have had his fingers crossed behind his back.) Harassment continued in Australia, where narcs tried to bust the band for various imagined vices.

After a month off, Fleetwood Mac swept through Europe riding in what they learned had been Hitler's private train, in order to avoid constant body searches at airport customs. At a June 1 mass rally at Munich's Olympic Riding Stadium, with Bob Marley and the Wailers opening, a hundred thousand fans gave Fleetwood Mac as thunderous a reception as they had ever known. From his drum chair, the best seat in the house, Mick Fleetwood looked

February 1981

Mick in Ghana, Africa, during the making of *The Visitor* album.

out at the crowd during "Go Your Own Way" and marveled that even the German riot cops were dancing. Triumph in Paris and the Low Countries led to five sold-out nights at London's Wembley Arena. From his hotel suite, Mick sent roadies out to scour London for lost angel Danny Kirwan. When he turned up at the hotel, he told Mick that he'd been sleeping on a park bench. He refused all Mick's offers of help.

Mick Fleetwood was the only band member who was enthusiastic about a live album from the *Tusk* tour. He insisted they document the shows, and material was recorded all over the world: "Monday Morning" in Japan; "Say You Love Me" in Wichita; "Dreams" from the Paris sound check; a psychedelic "Oh Well" from St. Louis, and so on. The group fleshed out *Fleetwood Mac Live* with a private performance for friends that included Stevie's flamboyant "Fireflies" and some gorgeous vocal harmonies on an homage to Brian Wilson's "The Farmer's Daughter." The last leg of the great *Tusk* campaign began in August 1980, in Florida, where someone threw a pair of crutches on stage,

"Stevie–You must be the most beautiful witch I could have ever met!" - M.F.

suggesting the miracles of Lourdes. The band had been playing for a year by then and was running on empty. Lindsey collapsed with a back problem and then heroically recovered. Stevie's nightly readings of "Landslide," redolent of melancholy and brave hope, were especially poignant. Meanwhile the entertainment press was full of lurid stories concerning the imminent breakup of Fleetwood Mac, citing romantic tension, drugs, and solo projects. All were flatly denied by the band. But at the final show of the tour, before a Hollywood Bowl audience of friends, colleagues, and the media, Lindsey leaned into the mike and announced, "This is our last concert...for a <u>very</u> long time."

A period of transition followed for Fleetwood Mac. *Tusk*, which had sold 4 million copies, was still judged a failure when measured in terms of *Rumours*, and amongst the band there were unspoken artistic recriminations as well. Worse, when the tour monies were totaled, the musicians realized that they been on the road for a year and had earned very little money because their overhead had been so awesome. They terminated Mick's career as band manager, and the five musicians began to spin off in tangential directions. Nineteen

eighty wasn't the end of Fleetwood Mac, but it was definitely the end of an era.

Stevie Nicks' first solo album, released the following year, was a huge success that established her as the unchallenged Queen of Rock. *Bella Donna* spawned two hit singles, "Stop Dragging My Heart Around" (with Tom Petty) and "Leather and Lace" (with Don Henley). She then assembled a strong band and put them on the road. Without Chris and Lindsey, Stevie didn't have a moment's rest on stage, but her momentum catapulted the spectacular single "Edge of Seventeen" to the top of the charts the year after that.

Mick Fleetwood, meanwhile, once again licked his wounds in Africa. This time, he took along some musician friends and state-of-the-art portable recording gear, and went to Ghana to explore and create links between African and Western rhythm. The result of this 1981 expedition was the wonderful album and video called *The Visitor*, released on RCA after Mick persuaded the company's enlightened president to foot the enormous bill. Mick's attempt to fuse Yoruba polyrhythms to rock's militant 4/4 proved to be way ahead of its time, as it

(Following page) Fleetwood Mac live.

127

the Set   1982

B   SECOND HAND NEWS
A   The CHAIN
E   DON'T STOP!
F   DREAMS
Em   OH WELL!
Am   RHIANNON
B   BROWN EYES
A   EYES OF THE WORLD
F   GYPSY
C   LOVE IN STORE
C   NOT THAT FUNNY (IS IT?)
       BRUSHES
       LANDSLIDE
(A) Dm TUSK
F   SARA
Am   HOLD ME!
       YOU MAKE LOVIN' FUN
       SO AFRAID
       BLUE LETTER
       GO YOU'RE OWN WAY
                BLUE LETTER
A   SISTERS
       SONGBIRD

• monitor.
• monitor back.

• monitor.
  same.

• monitor
  back

would be another five years before Paul Simon's *Graceland* managed to pull off anything remotely similar and make it a hit.

Lindsey Buckingham also went solo, releasing *Law and Order* in early 1982. This quirky album contained a Top Ten single, "Trouble," and was well received. Mick participated in the sessions, which produced a teasing chronicle of his African journey, not too sensitively titled "Bwana."

All the same, none of the musicians wanted Fleetwood Mac to wither. The power of their collective talents was too pure, too furious, to just let go. So in May 1981, the five musicians of Fleetwood Mac coalesced at an old castle in Herouville, France, to record the band's much-anticipated next album. There, the group that had been pronounced dead by media speculation found a new life.

Honky Chateau, as Elton John called it, is a famous recording studio in an elegant old country house nestled in misty landscape about sixty miles from Paris. It proved to be an appropriate address for Fleetwood Mac's attempt to recapture the mystical sonic frequency for which the group

Mirage tour rehearsal, 1982.

(Previous page) Mirage tour set list, 1982.

was most loved. The album recorded there, *Mirage*, was released in mid-1982 and immediately put Fleetwood Mac atop the charts once again. Christine's "Hold Me" was a worldwide hit, and Stevie's shining "Gypsy" (which was originally intended for *Bella Donna*) seemed to crystallize the essence of what Fleetwood Mac was supposed to be all about. Lindsey's "Oh Diane" was a hit single in England as well. A brief summer tour that year sent *Mirage* to the number-one spot on the charts—a great relief to the musicians who had been able to push *Tusk* only up to number four. Fleetwood Mac promoted its new music at massive outdoor shows like the U.S. Festival and through video saturation via a new twenty-four-hour cable channel that was calling itself Music Television – MTV. Like many of MTV's earliest heavy rotations, Fleetwood Mac's video imagery – surreal dunescapes for "Hold Me," gauzy boudoir ballet for "Gypsy" – proved to be unforgettable and very powerful.

Fleetwood Mac, for all its internal conflicts, was still very much a family, involving not only the five musicians but also various friends, lovers,

Fleetwood Mac at Le Chateau studio retreat near Paris for the recording of Mirage 1981.

colleagues, and crew. A pall was cast over this family when Stevie's best friend, Robin Anderson, died of leukemia in October 1982. Robin had been a beloved Mac associate for years; a distraught Stevie then threw herself into her work, releasing *The Wild Heart* later that year. "Stand Back" and "If Anyone Falls" cemented Stevie's abilities as a songwriter and performer, additional evidence that some artists do their most brilliant work while under the most horrendous stress.

Mick Fleetwood was also chasing the dream. He moved into a big ranch house in Malibu and established a raucous salon of pickers and players that metamorphosed into a transcendent bar band known as Mick Fleetwood's Zoo. The Zoo was fronted by second-generation rocker Billy Burnette, whose father and uncle, Dorsey and Johnny Burnette, were among the early Memphian founders of rock & roll. The Zoo was then a peripatetic organization whose members shifted in and out of muster. The Zoo backed up Lindsey when he appeared on *Saturday Night Live*; recorded an album (*I'm Not Me*) for RCA; and liked to play in selected saloons from Aspen to Trancas Canyon to Maui. When Stevie joined the

Mick and John, Mirage tour. September 1982.

band to sing "Rhiannon" at various gigs, they announced her as The Zooette. Other guests have included Christine McVie, Eddie Van Halen, guitarist Steve Cropper, Bob Seger, and Roy Orbison in one of his final performances.

Fleetwood Mac was dormant through the mid-1980s as its millionaire components pursued their separate muses. Mick Fleetwood hit the papers with a widely publicized bankruptcy in 1984.

Now Mick faced the difficult task of reuniting his scattered band. John McVie was semiretired on his boat in the Caribbean. Both Stevie Nicks and Lindsey Buckingham were engrossed in solo work. Christine McVie's long-awaited solo album had yielded a Top Ten single, "Got A Hold On Me," and she was said to be busy on a Hollywood film project.

But her soundtrack work proved to be the vehicle for the return of Fleetwood Mac. Asked to record Elvis's "Can't Help Falling in Love" for a movie, she recruited Lindsey to produce and play guitar; he in turn brought in the Fleetwood/McVie rhythm section. Suddenly, four-fifths of Fleetwood Mac found themselves in a recording studio in 1985. It felt right to everybody, and the old momentum quickly returned,

Fleetwood Mac in costume.

even if Stevie was preoccupied with the obligations of her solo work. While her bandmates began work, with Lindsey (who had shelved his solo album) producing, Stevie joined Bob Dylan and Tom Petty on a tour of Australia, then continued work on her own next album, Rock a Little. Her health began to deteriorate while she did a solo tour with a hot band that included Mick Fleetwood on percussion. Eventually, she spent a month fighting alcohol dependency at the Betty Ford Clinic, where she checked in under the name Sara. This experience inspired the song "Welcome to the Room, Sara," which Stevie sent to Fleetwood Mac when they were finishing the new album.

Tango in the Night, a gem of postmodern eighties sonic architecture, was released on 1987, the best-selling record Fleetwood Mac had issued in ten years. All three voices were strong on the airwaves, calling to each other like discarnate spirits in flight. "Everywhere" and "Little Lies" were classic Christine McVie. "Isn't It Midnight" and "Big Love" both glowed with pure, shimmering romance, while Stevie's "Seven Wonders" brought her impressive constituency back into

Fleetwood Mac's orbit. *Tango* immediately started to sell millions of CDs. It reached the Top Ten in America but really impacted in England, where it reached number one <u>twice</u> over the course of two years. Most of the musicians were thrilled to still be in a band that the world wanted to see again, that still had much left to offer.

One of them, however, wasn't so sure.

It was the summer of 1987, and *Tango in the Night* was a multiplatinum hit album. Fleetwood Mac seemed on the verge of yet another conquering world tour, until the other musicians noticed that Lindsey Buckingham seemed to be giving his notice in the press. He was telling friends and interviewers that he had done about all he could do with Fleetwood Mac, and just wanted to finish the solo album that he had interrupted to work on *Tango*. But the label intervened and a compromise was hammered out. Lindsey would play a ten-week tour and then he was free.

Once again word went out. Mac was back! The old team began to reassemble for another campaign. Roadies were hired, halls lined up, new lighting was designed, and a full schedule of concerts was booked. Then Lindsey backed out, letting the band know that he just wasn't prepared to tour. The other musicians asked for a meeting, held at Christine McVie's canyon house on August 7, 1987. Fleetwood Mac had held a lot of band meetings in its checkered past, but this was the stormiest. Lindsey told them he had given twelve years of his life to the cause, and now he had to get on with his life and music. He told them he didn't enjoy touring anymore, and that was it. Stevie Nicks reacted in pain and anger, the meeting ended badly, and Lindsey Buckingham left Fleetwood Mac the following day.

Fleetwood Mac lost no time in mending itself after Lindsey Buckingham's departure. They immediately recruited Billy Burnette from the Zoo to become the Band's frontman. He brought along his friend Rick Vito, a Los Angeles guitar pro who contributed expert re-creations of both Lindsey's and Peter Green's styles, as well as a chic flash of his own. The rhythm section was augmented for touring purposes by the sensational Ghanaian percussionist Isaac Asante, whose credits include Randy Weston and Paul Simon. He had met Mick during the latter's West African sojourn.

Fleetwood Mac publicity shot 1987.

138

"Lindsey, How Prophetic this
picture was to become. It was not long
after this that you walked out of
Fleetwood Mac to pursue the love of
your life, music, all on your very own.
No matter what was sometimes said
or done, your mark on Fleetwood Mac
will forever stand the test of time"
Love Mick

Evening News

MONDAY, M

35,836   PRICE 20p   Tel 031-225 2468

MIGHTY M

they're back . . .
better than ever

Rock giants Fleetwood Mac are back — and playing better than ever!

Ten years after their classic album "Rumours" took the world by storm, and five years after their last studio recording "Mirage", Mick Fleetwood, Christine McVie, John McVie, Stevie Nicks and Lindsey Buckingham delighted their millions of fans with a brilliant new LP, "Tango In The Night".

It was a worldwide smash!

Now a year later, that success has brought them out on the road for their first tour for years — and it's a sell-out, naturally.

their American guitarist, he had

What a Capital week for rock fans! The mighty Fleetwood Mac are back on stage in Edinburgh for two nights. The California-based band, who have been rocking the world for 21 years, are here with their new six-piece line-up — and judging by the rave reviews for their sell-out British tour, it's like they've never been away. So, Mac fans, let's make tonight a night to remember!

Mess" may have set the stage for "Tango In The Night".

Asked to record a version of the Elvis Presley ballad "Can't Help Falling In Love", she recruited Lindsey, Mick and John for the session.

"It was a very healthy exercise," Mick recalled. "It got us in the studio. It felt good, and it turned out really oil up the works, so to

"When you're contributing one-third of an album," Christine explained, "you have to think about what will go next to Stevie's singing or Lindsey's singing, or the character of their songs. You want a square meal, if you will.

"For instance, I wrote 'Isn't It Midnight?' because we needed something uptempo and driving, a guitar extravaganza. The idea is to give a of the five of us."

SPECIAL CONCERT EDITION

Evening News

35,837   PRICE 20p   Tel 031-225 2468

TUESDAY, MAY 10, 1988

MAC MAGIC

Rock giants take city by storm

What a Capital week for rock fans! The mighty Fleetwood Mac are back on stage in Edinburgh for two nights. The California-based band, who have been rocking the world for 21 years, are here with their new six-piece line-up — and it's like they've never been away. So, Mac fans, let's make tonight a night to remember!

Fleetwood Mac are back — and they are playing better than ever!

Ten years after their classic album "Rumours" took the world by storm, and five years after their last studio recording "Mirage", Mick Fleetwood, Christine McVie, John McVie, Stevie Nicks and Lindsey Buckingham delighted their millions of fans with a brilliant new LP, "Tango In The Night".

It was a worldwide smash!

Now a year later, that success has brought them out on the road for their first tour for years — and it's a sell-out, naturally.

Sadly, their American guitarist, Lindsey Buckingham, decided he had had enough of touring, so he left to concentrate on producing records.

Pictures from last night's show by JOE STEELE

Taking his place are two young Americans, Rick Vito and Billy Burnette.

The band have gone through many changes in the 21 turbulent years since they were a London-based blues band led by legendary guitarist Peter Green.

But Fleetwood Mac have never been a complacent band. And now with "Tango In The Night", they have again broken the mould.

Solo albums

The group have been involved in a variety of individual activities throughout the Eighties. All but founder-member John McVie have had solo albums.

Still, as Lindsey put it, "there wasn't much uncertainty that there would be an other Fleetwood Mac record. It was just a question of when."

"After 'Mirage', no-one actually talked about another Fleetwood Mac album for years", added Christine McVie, "but in the back our minds we were at least thinking about it. When we began work on this album (in late '85), we'd been out of each other's hair long enough to get together and enjoy it, which is what we did."

Extended break

Christine's work on the soundtrack for Blake Edwards' film "A Fine Mess" may have set the stage for "Tango In The Night".

Asked to record a version of the Elvis Presley ballad "Can't Help Falling In Love", she recruited Lindsey, Mick and John for the session.

"It was a very healthy exercise," Mick recalled. "It got us in the studio. It felt good, and it turned out really well. It helped oil up the works, so to speak."

And what was it like reuniting after an extended break?

"Suprisingly easy," Christine said. "It's like riding a bicycle, once you get back on the thing, you realise that it's not that difficult."

One thing which had changed, however, was the band's working environment. After being what Buckingham called "studio nomads" for "Mirage" and previous albums, they recorded "Tango's" basic tracks at Rumbo, in LA, and then retired to the newly-completed studio in Lindsey's Bel Air home for overdubs and mixing.

Extravaganza

What's more, in Buckingham and Richard Dashut, Fleetwood Mac's long-time co-producer/engineer, they had a production team with whom everyone was completely comfortable.

What they also have had is the singing and writing of Lindsey, Stevie and Christine.

Each has a distinct style: Stevie's spare, confessional, Lindsey's is rhythmically adventurous and Christine's by her own description is more "down the centre".

Yet "Tango In The Night" isn't a showcase for three solo artists — it's the work of a band.

"When you're contributing one-third of an album," Christine explained, "you have to think about what will go next to Stevie's singing or Lindsey's singing or the character of their songs. You want a square meal, if you will."

"Tango In The Night" offers a balance not only of musical styles, but of technology and feel.

Fresh ideas

"I think there has been some worry about the machines taking over," said Mick. "People are getting tired of music that's too perfect. There's no air in it at all and there's no emotion."

Fleetwood Mac preserved emotional content by putting the technology in the service of the music, instead of the other way around.

The result? An album of "fresh ideas," as Christine put it.

The fans may have been a little surprised by the album, Christine admitted.

"Then again, they may also be surprised that there is still a Fleetwood Mac at all . . .

The new boys . . . Billy Burnette and Rick Vito.

Looking good . . . and Stevie Nicks is in fine voice.

Six of the very best

ABOVE: What 3600 Edinburgh fans came to see . . . Fleetwood Mac rocking the Playhouse.

Six of the best — Christine McVie, John McVie, Stevie Nicks, Mick Fleetwood, Billy Burnette and Rick Vito.

RIGHT: Drummer Mick drives the band on, as Stevie's vocals and Billy's guitar take the spotlight.

Mick is celebrating 21 years . . .

The marvellous McVies . . . John and Christine.

MAC

WHAT DOES JOHN GIBSON

This was Fleetwood Mac, Mark XI, a red-hot touring band that played all over for the next four years. Billy revived the Green God's "Oh Well" in concert, and Rick Vito would chime the blues with touching fidelity on Pete's "I Loved Another Woman."

Stevie's great back-up singers joined the band, and "Stand Back" became an instant show-stopper. When this version of Fleetwood Mac went on the road in late 1987, Stevie Nicks was nervous about fronting a band that seemed unfamiliar to her without Lindsey, and she was recovering from a serious bout with the debilitating Epstein-Barr syndrome. But she earned glowing reviews, and gradually the tour assumed an informality and cavalier spirit that hadn't been visible for many years.

Mick had touch-sensitive drum pads sewn into his waistcoast and performed a marvelous high-tech tribal dance during "World Turning" that turned the show into a theatrically primitive rite as the masked Asante burned away behind him.

By 1988, this band was once

Billy age 7

"What can I say, Billy, the consummate pro from age seven to this very day. How lucky I am to have a friend like him!" - M.F.

BILLY BEAU

EXCLUSIVE ON Dot RECORDS

again putting on some of the best rock shows in the world. That spring, they sold out ten nights at London's Wembley Arena and played before members of the royal family, which the three English members of the band considered quite an honor. Later that year, the group released *Fleetwood Mac Greatest Hits*, a compendium of the band's best material since 1975, along with new songs by Stevie and Chris. Respectfully dedicated to Lindsey, with whom everyone had reconciled, this package appealed to a new generation of Mac fans eager to know what the lost era of seventies glamor and magic had been all about.

In 1990, Fleetwood Mac released *Behind the Mask*, its first modern album without Lindsey Buckingham. Despite Rick Vito's superb guitars and many strong songs (Chris's "Save Me" and "Skies the Limit," both written with her husband Eddie Quintela; Stevie's "Affairs of the Heart" and "Love Is Dangerous," written with Vito), the album was underrated in America. At home in England, however, *Mask* entered the charts at number one, and that

(Top left) Billy Burnette

(Top right) Billy in concert 1987.

(Below) Billy, Rick Vito and Mick on the road.

summer Fleetwood Mac sold out Wembley Stadium for the first time, playing before a couple hundred thousand fans, some of whom had been paying to see Fleetwood Mac for almost twenty-five years.

That summer's series of Euro shows also saw both Chris and Stevie announce in midtour that they would be leaving the band. Both women were wealthy and famous, and neither felt like continuing the pressure and the pace that went along with life in Fleetwood Mac. The two ladies reached this decision together, although both indicated they would continue to record with the band in the future. All this made the haunting lines Stevie delivered during "Landslide" – "Children get older, I'm getting older too" – all the more telling and poignant.

So Fleetwood Mac's Fall 1990 shows throughout America seemed like something of a farewell tour. Stevie's devotees came en masse in long chiffon gowns and flowing hair to throw their bouquets and stuffed animals on stage. And at the last show in Los Angeles, Lindsey mounted the stage to play some frenzied guitar, a fitting way for this edition of Fleetwood Mac to say goodbye. For now.

Tango tour 1987

(Far right) Publicity shot 1990

146

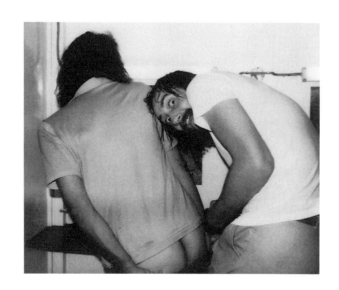

The End.

DISCOGRAPHY

PRE FLEETWOOD MAC DISCOGRAPHY

SINGLES

JOHN MAYALL & THE BLUESBREAKERS

CRAWLING UP A HILL

U.S. Release Date: Not Released

Catalogue Number:

U.K. Release Date: May 1964

Catalogue Number: Decca 11900

Producer: Mike Vernon

Tracks: Crawling Up A Hill / Mr. James

Features: John McVie

CROCODILE WALK

U.S. Release Date: Not Released

Catalogue Number:

U.K. Release Date: April 1965

Catalogue Number: Decca 12120

Producer: Tony Clarke

Tracks: Crocodile Walk / Blues City Shakedown

Features: John McVie

I'M YOUR WITCHDOCTOR

U.S. Release Date: October 1965

Catalogue Number: Immediate IM 502

U.K. Release Date: September 1965

Catalogue Number: Immediate IM 012

Producer: Jimmy Page

Tracks: I'm Your Witchdoctor / Telephone Blues

Features: John McVie

Note: Re-released in 1967 as Telephone Blues /
I'm Your Witchdoctor

U.K. Immediate IM 051

PARCHMAN FARM

U.K. Release Date: August 1966

Catalogue Number: London 20016

U.K. Release Date: August 1966

Catalogue Number: Decca 1249O

Producer: Mike Vernon

Tracks: Parchman Farm / Key To Love

Features: John McVie

JOHN MAYALL'S BLUESBREAKERS WITH PETER GREEN

LOOKING BACK

U.S. Release Date:

Catalogue Number:

U.K. Release Date: October 1966

Catalogue Number: Decca 125O6

Producer: Mike Vernon

Tracks: Looking Back / So Many Roads

Features: John McVie / Peter Green

JOHN MAYALL'S BLUESBREAKERS

SITTING IN THE RAIN

U.S. Release Date:

Catalogue Number:

U.K. Release Date: January 1967

Catalogue Number: Decca 12545

Producer: Mike Vernon

Tracks: Sitting In The Rain / Out Of Reach

Features: John McVie / Peter Green

THE BLUESBREAKERS

CURLY

U.S. Release Date: March 1967

Catalogue Number: London 20039

U.K. Release Date: March 1967

Catalogue Number: Decca 12588

Producer: Mike Vernon

Tracks: Curly / Rubber Duck

Features: John McVie / Peter Green

JOHN MAYALL'S BLUESBREAKERS

DOUBLE TROUBLE

U.S. Release Date:

Catalogue Number:

U.K. Release Date: June 1967

Catalogue Number: Decca 12621

Producer: Mike Vernon

Tracks: Double Trouble / It Hurts Me Too

Features: John McVie / Peter Green / Mick
Fleetwood

JOHN MAYALL'S BLUESBREAKERS WITH PAUL BUTTERFIELD

JOHN MAYALL'S BLUESBREAKERS WITH
PAUL BUTTERFIELD

U.S. Release Date:

Catalogue Number:

U.K. Release Date: April 1967

Catalogue Number: Decca DFE-R 8673

Producer: Mike Vernon

Tracks: All My Life / Riding On The L & N
Little By Little / Eagle Eye

Note: All tracks mono

Features: John McVie / Peter Green

THE CHEYNES

RESPECTABLE

U.S. Release Date: Not Released

Catalogue Number:

U.K. Release Date: December 1963

Catalogue Number: Columbia DB 7153

Producer: No Credit

Tracks: Respectable / It's Gonna Happen To You

Features: Mick Fleetwood

THE CHEYNES

GOING TO THE RIVER

U.S. Release Date: Not Released

Catalogue Number:

U.K. Release Date: October 1964

Catalogue Number: Columbia DB 7368

Producer: No Credit

Tracks: Going To The River / Cheyne-Re-La

Features: Mick Fleetwood

THE CHEYNES

DOWN AND OUT

U.S. Release Date: Not Released

Catalogue Number:

U.K. Release Date: February 1965

Catalogue Number: Columbia DB 7464

Producer: No Credit

Tracks: Down And Out / Stop Running Round

Features: Mick Fleetwood

BO STREET RUNNERS

BABY NEVER SAY GOODBYE

U.S. Release Date: Not Released

Catalogue Number:

U.K. Release Date: July 1965

Catalogue Number: Columbia DB 7640

Producer: No Credit

Tracks: Baby Never Say Goodbye / Get Out Of
My Way

Features: Mick Fleetwood

PETER B'S LOONERS

IF YOU WANNA BE HAPPY

U.S. Release Date: Not Released

Catalogue Number:

U.K. Release Date: March 1966

Catalogue Number: Columbia DB 7862

Producer: No Credit

Tracks: If You Wanna Be Happy / Jodrell Blues

Features: Mick Fleetwood / Peter Green

THE SHOTGUN EXPRESS

**I COULD FEEL THE WHOLE WORLD
TURN ROUND**

U.S. Release Date: Not Released

Catalogue Number:

U.K. Release Date: October 1966

Catalogue Number: Columbia DB 8025

Producer: No Credit

Tracks: I Could Feel The Whole World Turn
Round / Curtains

Features: Mick Fleetwood

THE SHOTGUN EXPRESS

FUNNY' 'COS NEITHER COULD I

U.S. Release Date: Not Released

Catalogue Number:

U.K. Release Date: February 1967

Catalogue Number: Columbia DB 8178

Producer: No Credit

Tracks: Funny 'Cos Neither Could I / Indian Thing

Features: Mick Fleetwood

EDDIE BOYD

IT'S SO MISERABLE TO BE ALONE

U.S. Release Date: Not Released

Catalogue Number:

U.K. Release Date:

Catalogue Number: Blue Horizon BH 1009

Features: John McVie / Peter Green

Note: (The rare 1000 series limited edition was
largely

distributed by mail order, and in connection with

R & B Monthly. Some copies were sold through

London specialist shops.)

FIVES COMPANY

SUNDAY FOR SEVEN DAYS

U.S. Release Date: Not Released

Catalogue Number:

U.K. Release Date: June 1966

Catalogue Number: Pye 7N 17118

Producer: No Credit

Tracks: Sunday For Seven Days / Big Kill

Features: Bob Brunning

FIVES COMPANY

SOME GIRLS

U.S. Release Date:

Catalogue Number:

U.K. Release Date: September 1966

Catalogue Number: Pye 7N 17162

Producer: No Credit

Tracks: Some Girls / Big Deal

Features: Bob Brunning

FIVES COMPANY

SESSION MAN

U.S. Release Date:

Catalogue Number:

U.K. Release Date: January 1967

Catalogue Number: Pye 7N 17199

Producer: No Credit

Tracks: Session Man / Rejection

Features: Bob Brunning

PRE FLEETWOOD MAC DISCOGRAPHY

ALBUMS

JOHN MAYALL AND THE BLUESBREAKERS

JOHN MAYALL PLAYS JOHN MAYALL

U.S. Release Date: Not Released

Catalogue Number:

U.K. Release Date: March 1965

Catalogue Number: Decca LK 4680

Producer: Tony Clarke

Features: John McVie

U.S. CD Polygram 820536- 2

U.K. CD London 820536-2

JOHN MAYALL WITH ERIC CLAPTON

BLUESBREAKERS

U.S. Release Date: July 1966

Catalogue Number: London PS 492

U.K. Release Date: May 1966

Catalogue Number: Decca SLK. 4804

Producer: Mike Vernon

Features: John McVie

U.S. CD Polygram 800086-2

U.K. CD Polygram 800086-2

JOHN MAYALL AND THE BLUESBREAKERS

A HARD ROAD

U.S. Release Date: February 1967

Catalogue Number: London PS 502

U.K. Release Date: February 1967

Catalogue Number: Decca SKL 4853

Producer: Mike Vernon

Features: John McVie / Peter Green

U.S. CD Polygram 820474- 2

U.K. CD London 820474-2

JOHN MAYALL'S BLUESBREAKERS

CRUSADE

U.S. Release Date: September 1967

Catalogue Number: London PS 592

U.K. Release Date: September 1967

Catalogue Number: Decca 5KL 4890

Producer: Mike Vernon

Features: John McVie

U.S. CD Polygram 820537- 2

U.K. CD London 820537-2

EDDIE BOYD

EDDIE BOYD AND HIS BLUES BAND

FEATURING PETER GREEN

U.S. Release Date: May 1967

Catalogue Number: London 4872

U.K. Release Date: May 1967

Catalogue Number: Decca LK 4872

Producer: Mike Vernon

Features: John McVie / Peter Green

VARIOUS ARTISTS

RAW BLUES

U.S. Release Date:

Catalogue Number: London PS 543

U.K. Release Date: April 1967

Catalogue Number: Decca SKLA 1220

Producer: Mike Vernon

Features: John McVie / Peter Green

U.S. CD Polygram 820479-2

U.K. CD Polygram 820479-2

VARIOUS ARTIST5

HISTORY OF BRITISH BLUES

U.S. Release Date:

Catalogue Number: Sire SAS 3170

U.K. Release Date: Not Released

Catalogue Number:

Producer: Mike Vernon

Features: John McVie / Peter Green / Mick Fleetwood

Christine Perfect

LONDON 22nd CUB SCOUT PACK

LONDON 22nd CUB SCOUT PACK

U.S. Release Date: Not Released

Catalogue Number:

U.K. Release Date:

Catalogue Number:

Producer:

Features: Bob Brunning

VARIOUS ARTISTS

BLUES ANYTIME VOLUME 2

U.S. Release Date: Not Released

Catalogue Number:

U.K. Release Date: 1969

Catalogue Number: Immediate IMLP 015

Producer:

Features: Jeremy Spencer

FLEETWOOD MAC DISCOGRAPHY

ALBUMS

PETER GREEN'S FLEETWOOD MAC

U.S. Release Date: June 1984

Catalogue Number: Epic BN 26402

U.K. Release Date: February 1968

Catalogue Number: Blue Horizon 7-63200

Producer: Mike Vernon

Tracks: My Heart Beat Like A Hammer / Merry Go Round / Long Gray Mare / Hellhound On My Trail / Shake Your Moneymaker / Looking For Somebody / No Place To Go / My Baby's Good To Me / I Loved Another Woman / Cold Black Night / The World Keep On Turning / Got To Move.

Reissues: U.K. CBS Embassy EMB 31036 (1973)

U.K. CBS 31494 (1977)

U.K. Impact / Line IMLP 4-00216 (Import) (white Vinyl) (1990)

MR. WONDERFUL

U.S. Release Date: Not Released

Catalogue Number:

U.K. Release Date: August 1968

Catalogue Number: Blue Horizon 7-63205

Producer: Mike Vernon

Tracks: Stop Messin'Round / I've Lost My Baby / Rollin'Man / Dust My Broom / Love That Burns / Doctor Brown / Need Your Love Tonight / If You Be My Baby / Evenin'Boogie / Lazy Poker Blues / Coming Home / Trying So Hard To Forget

Reissues: U.K. Castle Communications ESSLP 010 (1989)

U.K. CD Castle Communications ESSCD 010 (1989)

ENGLISH ROSE

U.S. Release Date: January 1969

Catalogue Number: Epic BN 26446

U.K. Release Date: Not Released

Catalogue Number:

Producer: Mike Vernon

Tracks: Stop Messin'Round / Jigsaw Puzzle Blues / Doctor Brown / Something Inside Of Me / Evenin'Boogie / Love That Burns / Black Magic Woman / I've Lost My Baby / One Sunny Day / Without You / Coming Home / Albatross.

Reissue: U.S. Columbia CSP P11651 (1973)

THE PIOUS BIRD OF GOOD OMEN

U.S. Release Date: Not Released

Catalogue Number:

U.K. Release Date: August 1969

Catalogue Number: Blue Horizon 7- 63215

Producer: Mike Vernon

Tracks: Need Your Love So Bad / Coming Home / Rambling Pony / The Big Boat / I Believe My Time Ain't Long / The Sun Is Shining / Albatross / Black Magic Woman / Just The Blues / Jigsaw Puzzle Blues / Looking For Somebody / Stop Messin'Round.

Reissue: U.K. CBS 32050 (1981)Note: Different cover

THEN PLAY ON

U.S. Release Date: October 1969

Catalogue Number: Reprise RS 6368

U.K. Release Date: September 1969

Catalogue Number: Reprise RSLP 9000

Producer: Fleetwood Mac

Tracks: Coming Your Way / Closing My Eyes / Fighting For Madge / When You Say / Show-Biz Blues / Under Way / One Sunny Day / Although The Sun is Shining / Rattlesnake Shake / Without You / Searching For Madge / My Dream / Like Crying / Before The Beginning.

Note: First U.S. release One Sunny Day, & Without You

tracks omitted. Second U.S. release When You Say, One Sunny Day, Without You, & My Dream tracks omitted, Oh Well Part I and 2 added.

Reissues: U.K. Reprise K 44103 (1971)

U.K. Reprise K 44103 () Note: Different cover

U.S. CD Reprise 6368 2 (1988)

U.K. CD WEA 927448 2 (1988)

BLUES JAM AT CHESS

U.S. Release Date: December 1969
Catalogue Number: Blue Horizon (Vol. 1, BH 4803. Vol. 2, BH 4805.)
U.K. Release Date: December 1969
Catalogue Number: Blue Horizon 7- 66227
Producer: Mike Vernon / Marshall Chess
Tracks: Watch Out / Ooh Baby / South Indiana-Take 1 / South Indiana-Take 2 / Last Night / Red Hot Jam / I'm Worried / I Held My Baby Last Night / Madison Blues / I Can't Hold Out / I Need Your Love / I Got The Blues / World's In A Tangle / Talk With You / Like It This Way / Someday Soon Baby / Hungry Country Girl / Black Jack Blues / Every Day I Have The Blues / Rockin'Boogie / Sugar Mama / Homework.
Note: U.S. release two separate albums

KILN HOUSE

U.S. Release Date: September 1970
Catalogue Number: Reprise RS 6408
U.K. Release Date: September 1970
Catalogue Number: Reprise RSLP 9004
Producer: Fleetwood Mac
Tracks: This Is The Rock / Station Man / Blood On The Floor / Hi Ho Silver / Jewel Eyed Judy / Buddy's Song / Earl Gray / One Together / Tell Me All The Things You Do / Mission Bell.
Reissues: U.K. Reprise K 54OO 1 (1971)
U.S. CD Reprise 6408 2
U.K. CD WEA 927453 2

THE ORIGINAL FLEETWOOD MAC

U.S. Release Date: November 1977
Catalogue Number. Sire SR 6045
U.K. Release Date: May 1971
Catalogue Number: CBS 63875
Producer: Mike Vernon
Tracks: Drifting / Leaving Town Blues / Watch Out / A Fool No More / Mean Old Fireman / Can't Afford To Do It / Fleetwood Mac / Worried Dream
Love That Woman / Allow Me One More Show / First Train Home / Rambling Pony No.2.
Reissue: U.K. Castle Communications ESSLP 026 (1990)
U.K. CD Castle Communications ESSCD 026 (1990)

FUTURE GAMES

U.S. Release Date: November 1971
Catalogue Number: Reprise RS 6465
U.K. Release Date: September 1971
Catalogue Number: Reprise K 44153
Producer: Fleetwood Mac
Tracks: Woman Of 1000 Years / Morning Rain / What A Shame / Future Games / Sands Of Time / Sometimes / Lay It All Down / Show Me A Smile.
U.S. CD Reprise 6465 2
U.K. CD WEA 927458 2

FLEETWOOD MAC GREATEST HITS

U.S. Release Date: Not Released
Catalogue Number:
U. K.. Release Date: November 1971
Catalogue Number: CBS 69011
Producer: Fleetwood Mac
Tracks: The Green Manalishi (With The Two Prong Crown) / Oh Well-Part 1 / Oh Well-part 2 / Shake Your Money Maker / Dragonfly / Black Magic Woman / Albatross / Man Of The World / Stop Messin' Round / Love That Burns.
Reissues: U.K CBS S 6901 (   )Note: Standard gatefold sleeve
U.K- CBS 460704 1 (1988)
U.K. CD CBS 460704 2 (1988)

BARE TREES

U.S. Release Date: March 1972
Catalogue Number: Reprise MS 2080
U.K. Release Date: August 1972
Catalogue Number: Reprise K 44181
Producer: Fleetwood Mac
Tracks: Child Of Mine / The Ghost / Homeward Bound / Sunny Side Of Heaven / Bare Trees / Sentimental Lady / Danny's Chant / Spare Me A Little Of Your Love / Dust / Thoughts On A Grey Day.
Reissue: U.S. Reprise MSK 2278
U.S. CD Reprise 2278 2
U.K. CD WEA INTL CD 2278 2

PENGUIN

U.S. Release Date: March 1973
Catalogue Number: Reprise MS 2138
U.K. Release Date: May 1973
Catalogue Number: Reprise K44235
Producer: Fleetwood Mac / Martin Birch
Tracks: Remember Me / Bright Fire /

Dissatisfied / (I'm A)Road Runner / The Derelict / Revelation / Did You Ever Love Me / Night Watch / Caught In The Rain
U.S. CD Reprise 2138 2
U.K. CD

MYSTERY TO ME

U.S. Release Date: October 1973
Catalogue Number: Reprise MS 2158
U.K. Release Date: January 1974
Catalogue Number: Reprise K44248
Producer: Fleetwood Mac / Martin Birch
Tracks: Emerald Eyes / Believe Me / Just Crazy Love / Hypnotized / Forever / Keep On Going / The City / Miles Away / Somebody / The Way I Feel / For Your Love / Why.
Reissue: U.S. Reprise MSK 2279
U.S. CD Reprise 9 25982
U.K. CD

HEROES ARE HARD TO FIND

U.S. Release Date: September 1974
Catalogue Number: Reprise MS 2196
U.K. Release Date: September 1974
Catalogue Number: Reprise K 54026
Producer: Fleetwood Mac / Bob Hughes
Tracks: Heroes Are Hard To Find / Coming Home / Angel / Bermuda Triangle / Come A Little Bit Closer / She's Changing Me / Bad Loser / Silver Heals / Prove Your Love / Born Enchanter / Safe Harbour,
U.S. CD Reprise 2196 2
U.K. CD WEA INTL 2196 2

FLEETWOOD MAC

U.S. Release Date: July 1975
Catalogue Number: Reprise MS 2225
U.K. Release Date: August 1975
Catalogue Number: Reprise K 54043
Producer: Fleetwood Mac / Keith Olsen
Tracks: Monday Morning / Warm Ways / Blue Letter / Rhiannon / Over My Head / Crystal / Say You Love Me / Landslide / World Turning / Sugar Daddy / I'm So Afraid.
Note: U.K. Limited edition white vinyl Reprise K 54043
Reissue: U.S. Reprise 2281
U.S. CD Reprise 2281 2 (1983)
U.K. CD Reprise 254043 (1983)

RUMOURS

U.S. Release Date: February 1977
Catalogue Number: Warner Brothers BSK 3010
U.K. Release Date: February 1977
Catalogue Number: Warner Brothers K 56344
Producer: Fleetwood Mac / Richard Dashut / Ken Caillat / Chris Morris
Tracks: Second Hand News / Dreams / Never Going Back Again / Don't Stop / Go Your Own Way / Songbird / The Chain / You Make Loving Fun / I Don't Want To Know / Oh Daddy / Gold Dust Woman.
Note: U.K. Limited edition white vinyl Reprise (Import) Warner
Brothers 56344
U.K. His Masters Voice C88 1-1 (1988)Limited Edition Box Set 3500
copies, includes 12 page booklet
U.S. CD Warner Brothers 3010 2 (1983)
U.K. CD Warner Brothers 256344 (1983)

TUSK

U.S. Release Date: October 1979
Catalogue Number: Warner Brothers 3350
U.K. Release Dale: October 1979
Catalogue Number: Warner Brothers K 66088
Producer: Fleetwood Mac (Special thanks to Lindsey Buckingham) /
Richard Dashut / Ken Caillat
Over & Over / The Ledge / Think About Me /
Tracks: Save Me A Place / Sara / What Makes You Think Your The One / Storms / That's All For Everyone / Not That Funny / Sisters Of The Moon / Angel / That's Enough For Me / Brown Eyes / Never Make Me Cry / I Know I'm Not Wrong / Honey Hi / Beautiful Child / Walk A Thin Line / Tusk / Never Forget.
U.S. CD Warner Brothers 2694 2 (1987)
U.K. CD Warner Brothers 266088 (1987)

LIVE

U.S. Release Date: December 1980
Catalogue Number: Warner Brothers 3500
U.K. Release Date:December 1980
Catalogue Number: Warner Brothers K 66097
Producer: Fleetwood Mac / Ken Caillat / Richard Dashut
Tracks: Monday Morning / Say You Love Me / Dreams / Oh Well / Over & Over / Sara / Not That Funny / Never Going Back Again /

Landslide / Fireflies / Over My Head / Rhiannon / Don't Let Me Down Again / One More Night / Go Your Own Way / Don't Stop / I'm So Afraid / The Farmer's Daughter.
U.S. CD Warner Brothers 3500 2
U.K. CO Warner Brothers 927410 2

MIRAGE

U.S. Release Date: June 1982
Catalogue Number: Warner Brothers 23607
U.K. Release Date: June 1982
Catalogue Number: Warner Brothers K 6952
Producer: Lindsey Buckingham / Richard Dashut / Ken Caillat / Fleetwood Mac
Tracks: Love In Store / Can't Go Back / That's Alright / Book Of Love / Gypsy / Only Over You / Empire State / Straight Back / Hold Me / Oh Diane / Eyes Of The World / Wish You Were Here.
U.S. CD Warner Brothers 23607 2 (1983)
U.K. CD Warner Brothers 256952 (1983)
Reissue: U.K. CD Warner Brothers K 256952 (1989)

TANGO IN THE NIGHT

U.S. Release Date: April 1987
Catalogue Number: Warner Brothers 1 -25471
U.K. Release Date: April 1987
Catalogue Number: Warner Brothers WX 65
Producer: Lindsey Buckingham / Richard Dashut
Tracks: Big Love / Seven Wonders / Everywhere / Caroline / Tango In The Night / Mystified / Little Lies / Family Man / Welcome To The Room...Sara / Isn't It Midnight / When I See You Again / You And I, Part 11
U.S. CD Warner Brothers 254712 (1987)
U.K. CD Warner Brothers 9254712 (1987)

GREATEST HITS

U.S. Release Date: November 1988
Catalogue Number: Warner Brothers 25801 - 1
U.K. Release Date: November 1988
Catalogue Number: Warner Brothers WX 221
Producer: Greg Ladanyi / Fleetwood Mac
Rhiannon / Don't Stop / Go Your Own Way / Hold Me / Everywhere / Gypsy / As Long As You Follow / Say You Love Me / Dreams / Little Lies / Sara / Tusk / No Questions Asked
U.S. CD Warner Brothers 25838 2 (1988)
Note: U.S. CD has 3 additional tracks-You

Make Loving Fun / Big Love / Over My Head
U.K. CD Warner Brothers 925838 2 (1988)
Note: U.K. CD has 4 additional tracks-You Make Loving Fun / Big Love / Over My Head / Oh Diane

BEHIND THE MASK

U.S. Release Date: April 1990
Catalogue Number: Warner Brothers 1-266111
U.K. Release Date: April 1990
Catalogue Number: Warner Brothers WX 335
Producer: Greg Ladanyi / Fleetwood Mac
Tracks: Skies The Limit / Love Is Dangerous / In The Back Of My Mind / Do You Know / Save Me / Affairs Of The Heart / When The Sun Goes Down / Behind The Mask / Stand On The Rock / Hard Feelings / Freedom / When It Comes To Love / The Second Time.
U.S. CD Warner Brothers 9-26111-2 (1990)
U.K. CD Warner Brothers 7599261112 (1990)
U.S. CD Limited Edition Box Warner Brothers 9 26206-2 (1990)
U.K. CD Limited Edition Box Warner Brothers 759926206 2 (1990)

FLEETWOOD MAC DISCOGRAPHY REISSUE ALBUMS

BLACK MAGIC WOMAN

U.S. Epic EG 30632 (l971)
U. K. Not Released
Note: Reissue of Peter Green's Fleetwood Mac and English Rose

FLEETWOOD MAC IN CHICAGO

U.S. Blue Horizon BH 3801 (1971)
U.K. Not Released
Note: Reissue of Blues Jam At Chess

FLEETWOOD MAC / ENGLISH ROSE

U.S. Epic 33740 (1974)
U.K. Not Released
Note: Reissue of Peter Green's Fleetwood Mac and English Rose

FLEETWOOD MAC IN CHICAGO

U.S. Sire SASH 3715-2 (1975)
U.S. Reissue Sire SASH 2XS 6009
U.K. Not Released
Note: Reissue of Blues Jam At Chess

VINTAGE YEARS

U.S. Release Date: March 1971
Catalogue Number: Sire SASH 3706-2
U.K. Release Date: March 1977
Catalogue Number: CBS 88227
Producer: Mike Vernon
Tracks: Black Magic Woman / Coming Home / Rambling Pony /
Something Inside Of Me / Dust My Broom / The Sun Is Shining / Albatross / Just The Blues / Evening Boogie / The Big Boat / Jigsaw Puzzle Blues / I've Lost My Baby / Doctor Brown / Need Your Love So Bad / Looking For Somebody / Need Your Love Tonight / Shake Your Moneymaker / Man Of The World / Stop Messin' Round / Rollin' Man / Love That Burns / If You Be My Baby / Lazy Poker Blues / Trying So Hard To Forget.
U.S. Reissue Sire 2XS 6006
U.K. Reissue CBS 22122

THE ORIGINAL FLEETWOOD MAC / ENGLISH ROSE

U.S. Not Released
U.K. CBS 81308 / 9
U.K. Reissue CBS 22025 (1976)
Note: Reissue of the Original Fleetwood Mac and English Rose

ALBATROSS

U.S. Release Date: Not Released
Catalogue Number:
U.K. Release Date: August 1977
Catalogue Number: Embassy S CBS 31569
Producer: Mike Vernon
Tracks: Side One: FLEETWOOD MAC Albatross / Rambling Pony / I Believe My Time Ain't Long / Doctor Brown / Stop Messin' Round / Love That Burns / Jigsaw Puzzle Blues / Need Your Love Tonight.
Side Two: CHRISTINE PERFECT I'd Rather Go Blind / Crazy' Bout You Baby / And That's Saying A Lot / I'm On My Way / No Road Is The Right Road / Let Me Go (Leave Me Alone) / I'm Too Far Gone (To Turn Around) / When You Say.
U.K. CD Columbia 31569 (1991)

MAN Of THE WORLD

U.S. Release Date: Not Released
Catalogue Number:

U.K. Release Date: 1978
Catalogue Number: Reprise REP 44138
Producer: Fleetwood Mac
Tracks: Oh Well / Dragonfly / Rattlesnake Shake / World In Harmony / The Green Manalishi / Searching for Madge / Before The Beginning / The Purple Dancer / Fighting For Madge / Coming Your Way.

BLACK MAGIC WOMAN

U.S. Release Date: Not Released
Catalogue Number:
U.K. Release Date: February 1980
Catalogue Number: CBS 3 1980
Producer: Mike Vernon /*Mike Vernon and Marshall Chess
Tracks: Black Magic Woman / Coming Home / Lazy Poker Blues / Something Inside Of Me / Evening Boogie / If You Be My Baby / Without You / Rockin' Boogie / Need Your Love So Bad / Rollin' Man / Dust My Broom / I've Lost My Baby / The Big Boat / Shake Your Moneymaker / The Sun Is Shining / *Last Night
U.K. CD CBS

LIVE IN BOSTON

U.S. Release Date: Not Released
Catalogue Number:
U.K. Release Date: February 1985
Catalogue Number: Shanghai HAI 107
Producer: No Credit
Tracks: Oh Well / Like It This Way / World In Harmony / Only You / Black Magic Woman / Jumping At Shadows / Can't Hold On /
Note: All tracks live
Reissue: U.K. Castle Communications CLACP 152 (1988)
U.K. Impact / Line IMLP 4-00129 Import white vinyl (1990)
U.K. CD Castle Communications CLACD 152 (1989)

JUMPING AT SHADOWS

U.S. Release Date: May 1985
Catalogue Number: Varrick Records VR020
U.K. Release Date: Not Released
Catalogue Number:
Producer: No Credit
Tracks: The same as Live in Boston Shanghai HAI 107 (U.K.)

25-3P-114

Epic

English Rose

Fleetwood Mac

CERULEAN

U.S. Release Date: Not Released

Catalogue Number:

U.K. Release Date: August 1985

Catalogue Number: Shanghai HAI 300

Producer: No Credit

Tracks: Madison Blues / Sandy Mary / Stranger Blues / Great Balls Of Fire / Jenny Jenny / Got To Move / Oh Baby / Teenage Darling / Loving Kind / Tutti Frutti / Rattlesnake Shake / Keep A Knocking / Red Hot Mama / Green Manalishi.

Note: All tracks live

RATTLESNAKE SHAKE

U.S. Release Date: Not Released

Catalogue Number:

U.K. Release Date: October 1985

Catalogue Number: Shanghai HAI 400

Producer: No Credit

Tracks: Oh Well / World In Harmony / Sandy Mary / Black Magic Woman / Madison Blues / Rattlesnake Shake / Green Manalishi

Note: CD release only-All tracks live

LONDON LIVE 68'

U.S. Release Date: Not Released

Catalogue Number:

U.K. Release Date: November 1986

Catalogue Number: Thunderbolt THBL 1-038

Producer: No Credit

Tracks: Got To Move / I Held My Baby Last Night / My Baby's Sweet / My Baby's A Good 'Un / Don't Know Which Way To Go / Buzz Me / The World Keeps On Turning / How Blue Can You Get / Bleeding Heart.

U.K. CD Thunderbolt CDTB 1 -038 (1987)

Note: All tracks live

THE COLLECTION

U.S. Release Date: Not Released

Catalogue Number:

U.K. Release Date: July 1987

Catalogue Number: Castle Communications CCSLP 157

Producer: No Credit

Tracks: Shake Your Moneymaker / Long Grey Mare / I Loved Another Woman / Got To Move / World Keep On Turning / Black Magic Woman / Need Your Love So Bad / Doctor Brown / Need

Your Love Tonight / Love That Burns / Lazy Poker Blues. / Dust My Broom / Drifting / Fleetwood Mac / Love That Woman / I've Lost My Baby / Man Of The World / Someone's Gonna Get The r Head Kicked In Tonight / Watch Out / Homework / Rockin' Boogie / Jigsaw Puzzle Blues / Albatross.

U.K. CD Castle Communications CCSCD 157

THE EARLY YEARS

U.S. Release Date: 1988

Catalogue Number: Pair Records

U.K. Release Date: Not Released

Catalogue Number:

Producer: No Credit

Tracks: Madison Blues / Sandy Mary / Great Balls Of Fire / Jenny Jenny / Oh Baby / Teenage Darling / Tutti Frutti / Keep A Knocking.

U.S. CD Pair Records SCD 4918 (1988)

Note: All tracks live

GREATEST HITS LIVE

U.S. Release Date: Not Released

Catalogue Number:

U.K. Release Date: May 1988

Catalogue Number: Commander 2148217

Producer: No Credit

Tracks: Oh Well / Black Magic Woman / World In Harmony / Like It This Way / Only You / Jumping At Shadows / Can't Hold Out / The Green Manalishi / Red Hot Mamma / Stranger Blues.

U.K. CD Commander 2448217

Note: All tracks live

ROOTS-THE ORIGINAL LIVE IN CONCERT

U.S. Release Date: 1988

Catalogue Number: Pair Records PDL 2- 1208

U.K. Release Date: Not Released

Catalogue Number:

Producer: No Credit

Tracks: Madison Blues / Sandy Mary / Stranger Blues / Great Balls Of Fire / Jenny Jenny / Got To Move / Oh Baby / Teenage Daring / Loving Kind / Tutti Frutti / Rattlesnake Shake / Keep A Knocking / Red Hot Momma / The Green Manalishi.

U.S. CD Pair Records PCD 2- 1208

Note: All tracks live

FLEETWOOD MAC LIVE

U.S. Release Date: 1988

Catalogue Number: Commander 99011 (CD Release only)

U.K. Release Date: Not Released-Available as an import

Catalogue Number:

Producer: No Credit

Tracks: Keep A Knocking / Red Hot Mamma / Green Manalishi / Madison Blues / Sandy Mary / Stranger Blues / Great Balls OF Fire / Jenny Jenny / Got To Move / Oh Baby /

OH WELL

U.S. Release Date: Not Released

Catalogue Number:

U.K. Release Date: November 1989

Catalogue Number: Mainline 264 8241

Producer: No Credit

Tracks: Keep A Knocking / Red Hot Mama / Green Manalishi / Madison Blues / Sandy Mary / Stranger Blues / Great Balls Of Fire / Jenny Jenny / Got To Move / Oh Baby / Teenage Darling / Loving Kind / Tutti Frutti / Oh Well / Black Magic Woman / World In Harmony / Like It This Way / Only You / Jumping At Shadows / Can't Hold On / Rattlesnake Shake.

U.K. CD Mainline 264 824 22

LOOKING BACK AT FLEETWOOD MAC

U.S. Release Date: Not Released

Catalogue Number:

U.K. Release Date: September 1989

Catalogue Number: Pickwick SHM 3268

Producer: No Credit

Tracks: Albatross / Looking For Somebody / My Baby's Good To Me / I Loved Another Woman / If You Be My Baby / Without You / Jigsaw Puzzle Blues / Black Magic Woman / Need Your Love So Bad / Love That Burns / My Heart Beats Like A Hammer / I Believe My Time Ain't Long / Shake Your Moneymaker / World Keeps On Turning / Stop Messin' Round / Coming Home

U.K. CD Pickwick PWK S533

THE BLUES COLLECTION

U.S. Release Date: Not Released

Catalogue Number:

U.K. Release Date: April 1989

Catalogue Number: Castle Communications CCSLP 216

Producer: No Credit

Tracks: Green Manalishi (Shortened version) / Sandy Mary / Jumping At Shadows / Oh Well / Black Magic Woman / World In Harmony / Like It This Way / Rattlesnake Shake / Got To Move / Madison Blues / Teenage Darling / Red Hot Mamma

U.K. CD Castle Communications CCSCD 216

Note: All Tracks live

THE BLUES YEARS

U.S. Release Date: Not Released

Catalogue Number:

U.K. Release Date: February 1991

Catalogue Number: Castle Communications ESBLP 138

Producer: Various

Tracks: My Heart Beat Like A Hammer / Merry Go Round / Long Grey Mare / Hell Hound On My Trail / Shake Your Moneymaker / Looking For Somebody / No Place To Go / My Baby's Good To Me / I Loved Another Woman / Cold Black Night / The World Keep On Turning / Got To Move / Stop Messin' Round / Coming Home / Rollin' Man / Dust My Broom / Love That Burns / Doctor Brown / Need Your Love Tonight / If You Be My Baby / Evenin' Boogie / Lazy Poker Blues / I've Lost My Baby / Trying So Hard To Forget / I Believe My Time Ain't Long / Ramblin' Pony / Black Magic Woman / The Sun Is Shining / Need Your Love So Bad / Albatross / Jigsaw Puzzle Blues / Man Of The World / Somebody's Gonna Get Their Head Kicked In Tonight / Watch Out / Worried Dream / Fleetwood Mac / First Train Home / Mean Old Fireman / Allow Me One More Show / Just The Blues / The Big Boat / I'd Rather Go Blind / Watch Out (2nd version) / Homework / I Can't Hold Out / Like It This Way / Last Night / I'm Worried / World's In A Tangle.

U.K. CD Castle Communications ESBCD 138 (1991)

Note: 5 album box set, and 3 CD box set

LIKE IT THIS WAY

U.S. Release Date: Not Released

Catalogue Number:

U.K. Release Date: May 1991

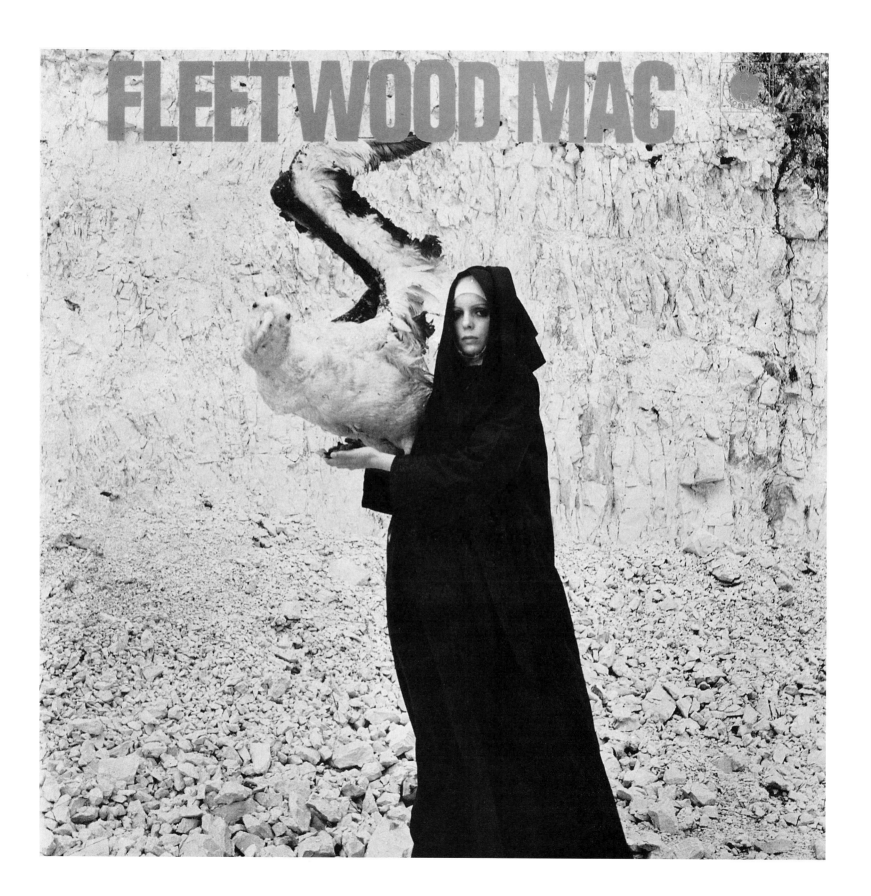

Catalogue Number: Elite 008CD (CD release only)

Producer: Various

Tracks: Lazy Poker Blues / Something Inside Of Me / Evening Boogie / Rockin' Boogie / Dust My Broom / Rollin' Man / Merry Go' Round / Hell hound On My Trail / Last Night / Need Your Love Tonight / Rambling Pony / I Can't Hold Out / Like It This Way / Homework / Cold Black Night / The Big Boat / Just The Blues / Dragonfly / Trying So Hard To Forget

ORIGINAL MASTER RECORDING'S

FLEETWOOD MAC

U.S. Mobile Fidelity MFSL 1 - 012

U.K. Not Released

RUMOURS

U.S. Warner Brothers / Nauticlus NR8

U K. Not Released

MIRAGE

U.S. Mobile Fidelity MFSL 1 - 119

U.K. Not Released

MISCELLANEOUS

LIMITED EDITION INTERVIEW PICTURE DISK FLEETWOOD MAC

(Mick Fleetwood interviewed)

U.S. Not Released

U.K. Baktabak BAK 2126 (1989)

LIMITED EDITION CD BOX SET FLEETWOOD MAC THE INTERVIEW

U.S. Not Released

U.K. CID Productions CID 016

CASSETTE ONLY RELEASES

RUMOURS / FLEETWOOD MAC

U.S.

U.K. Warner Brothers K 466103 (1982)

PETER GREEN'S FLEETWOOD MAC / THE PIOUS BIRD OF GOOD OMEN

U.S. Not Released

U.K. CBS 4022163

FLEETWOOD MAC DISCOGRAPHY

SINGLES

I BELIEVE MY TIME AIN'T LONG

U.S. Release Date: Not Released

Catalogue Number:

U.K. Release Date: November 1967

Catalogue Number: Blue Horizon 3051

Producer: Mike Vernon

Tracks: I Believe My Time Ain't Long / Rambling Pony

BLACK MAGIC WOMAN

U.S. Release Date: June 1968

Catalogue Number: Epic 5- 10351

U.K. Release Date: March 1968

Catalogue Number: Blue Horizon 57-3 138

Producer: Mike Vernon

Tracks: U.S. Black Magic Woman / Long Grey Mare

U.K. Black Magic Woman / The Sun Is Shining

NEED YOUR LOVE SO BAD

U.S. Release Date: Not Released

Catalogue Number:

U.K. Release Date: July 1968

Catalogue Number: Blue Horizon 57-3139

Producer: Mike Vernon

Tracks: Need Your Love So Bad / Stop Messin' Round

NEED YOUR LOVE SO BAD

U.S. Release Date: August 1968

Catalogue Number: Epic 5 -10386

U.K. Release Date: July 1969

Catalogue Number: Blue Horizon 57-3157

Producer: Mike Vernon

Tracks: Need Your Love So Bad / No Place To Go

ALBATROSS

U.S. Release Date: January 1969

Catalogue Number: Epic 5 -10436

U.K. Release Date: November 1968

Catalogue Number: Blue Horizon 57 -3145

Producer: Mike Vernon

Tracks: Albatross / Jigsaw Puzzle Blues

MAN OF THE WORLD

U.S. Release Date: Not Released

Catalogue Number:

U.K. Release Date: April 1969

Catalogue Number: Immediate IM 08O

Producer: Mike Vernon / Fleetwood Mac

Tracks: Man Of The World / Somebody's Gonna Get Their Head Kicked In Tonight (By Earl Vince And The Valiants - A Fleetwood Mac guise)

RATTLESNAKE SHAKE

U.S. Release Date: September 1969

Catalogue Number: Reprise 0860

U.K. Release Date: Not Released

Catalogue Number:

Producer: Fleetwood Mac

Tracks: Rattlesnake Shake / Coming Your Way

OH WELL

U.S. Release Date: November 1969

Catalogue Number: Reprise REP 0883

U.K. Release Date: September 1969

Catalogue Number: Reprise RS 27000

Producer: Fleetwood Mac

Tracks: Oh Well (Part 1) / Oh Well (Part 2)

THE GREEN MANALISHI (WITH THE TWO PRONG CROWN)

U.S. Release Date: June 1970

Catalogue Number: Reprise REP 0925

U.K. Release Date: May 1970

Catalogue Number: Reprise RS 27007

Producer: Fleetwood Mac

Tracks: The Green Manalishi (With The Two Pronged Crown) / World In Harmony

JEWEL EYED JUDY

U.S. Release Date: January 1971

Catalogue Number: Reprise REP 0984

U.K. Release Date: Not Released

Catalogue Number:

Producer: Fleetwood Mac

Tracks: Jewel Eyed Judy / Station Man

DRAGONFLY

U.S. Release Date: Not Released

Catalogue Number:

U.K. Release Date: March 1971

Catalogue Number: Reprise RS 27010

Producer: Fleetwood Mac

Tracks: Dragonfly / Purple Dancer

SANDS OF TIME

U.S. Release Date: November 1971

Catalogue Number: Reprise REP 1057

U.K. Release Date: Not Released

Catalogue Number:

Producer: Fleetwood Mac

Tracks: Sands Of Time / Lay It All Down

SENTIMENTAL LADY

U.S. Release Date: May 1972

Catalogue Number: Reprise REP 1093

U.K. Release Date: Not Released

Catalogue Number:

Producer: Fleetwood Mac

Tracks: Sentimental Lady / Sunny Side Of Heaven

SPARE ME A LITTLE

U.S. Release Date: Not Released

Catalogue Number:

U.K. Release Date: August 1972

Catalogue Number: Reprise K 14914

Producer: Fleetwood Mac

Tracks: Spare Me A Little / Sunny Side Of Heaven

REMEMBER ME

U.S. Release Date: May 1973

Catalogue Number: Reprise REP 1159

U.K. Release Date: Not Released

Catalogue Number:

Producer: Fleetwood Mac / Martin Birch

Tracks: Remember Me / Dissatisfied

DID YOU EVER LOVE ME

U.S. Release Date: August 1973

Catalogue Number: Reprise REP 1172

U.K. Release Date: June 1973

Catalogue Number: Reprise K 14280

Producer: Fleetwood Mac / Martin Birch

Tracks: U.S. Did You Ever Love Me / Revelation

U.K. Did You Ever Love Me / The Derelict

FOR YOUR LOVE

U.S. Release Date: December 1973

Catalogue Number: Reprise REP 1188

U.K. Release Date: March 1974

Catalogue Number: Reprise K 14315

Producer: Fleetwood Mac / Martin Birch

Tracks: For Your Love / Hypnotized

HEROES ARE HARD TO FIND

U.S. Release Date: September 1974

Catalogue Number: Reprise RPS 1317

U.K. Release Date: February 1975

Catalogue Number: Reprise K 14388

Producer: Fleetwood Mac / Bob Hughes

Tracks: Heroes Are Hard To Find / Born Enchanter

OVER MY HEAD

U.S. Release Date: September 1975

Catalogue Number: Reprise RPS 1339

U.K. Release Date: February 1976

Catalogue Number: Reprise K 14413

Producer: Fleetwood Mac / Keith Olsen

Tracks: Over My Head (Edit) / I'm So Afraid

WARM WAYS

U.S. Release Date: Not Released

Catalogue Number:

U.K. Release Date: October 1975

Catalogue Number: Reprise K 14403

Producer: Fleetwood Mac / Keith Olsen

Tracks: Warm Ways / Blue Letter

RHIANNON

U.S. Release Date: January 1976

Catalogue Number: Reprise RPS 1345

U.K. Release Date: April 1976

Catalogue Number: Reprise K 14430

Producer: Fleetwood Mac / Keith Olsen

Tracks: Rhiannon / Sugar Daddy

SAY YOU LOVE ME

U.S. Release Date: June 1976

Catalogue Number: Reprise RPS 1356

U.K. Release Date: September 1976

Catalogue Number: Reprise K 14447

Producer: Fleetwood Mac / Keith Olsen

Tracks: Say You Love Me / Monday Morning

GO YOUR OWN WAY

U.S. Release Date: December 1976

Catalogue Number: Warner Brothers WBS 8304

U.K. Release Date: January 1977

Catalogue Number: Warner Brothers K 16872

Producer: Fleetwood Mac / Richard Dashut / Ken Caillat

Tracks: Go Your Own Way / Silver Springs

DREAMS

U.S. Release Date: April 1977

Catalogue Number: Warner Brothers WBS 8371

U.K. Release Date: June 1977

Catalogue Number: Warner Brothers K 16969

Producer: Fleetwood Mac / Richard Dashut / Ken Caillat

Tracks: Dreams / Songbird

DON'T STOP

U.S. Release Date: July 1977

Catalogue Number: Warner Brothers WBS 8413

U.K. Release Date: April 1977

Catalogue Number: Warner Brothers K 16930

Producer: Fleetwood Mac / Richard Dashut / Ken Caillat

Tracks: U.S. Don't Stop / Never Going Back Again

U.K. Don't Stop / Gold Dust Woman

YOU MAKE LOVING FUN

U.S. Release Date: October 1977

Catalogue Number: Warner Brothers WBS 8483

U.K. Release Date: September 1977

Catalogue Number: Warner Brothers K 17013

Producer: Fleetwood Mac / Richard Dashut / Ken Caillat

Tracks: U.S. You Make Loving Fun / Gold Dust Woman

U.K. You Make Loving Fun / Never Going Back Again

TUSK

U.S. Release Date: October 1979

Catalogue Number: Warner Brothers WBS 49077

U.K. Release Date: September 1979

Catalogue Number: Warner Brothers K 1 7468

Producer: Fleetwood Mac (Special thanks to L. Buckingham) / Richard Dashut / Ken Caillat

Tracks: Tusk / Never Make Me Cry

SARA

U.S. Release Date: December 1979

Catalogue Number: Warner Brothers WBS 49150

U.K. Release Date: December 1979

Catalogue Number: Warner Brothers K 17533

Producer: Fleetwood Mac (Special thanks to L. Buckingham) / Richard Dashut / Ken Caillat

Tracks: Sara / That's Enough for Me

NOT THAT FUNNY

U.S. Release Date: Not Released

Catalogue Number:

U.K. Release Date: February 1980

Catalogue Number: Warner Brothers K 17577

Producer: Fleetwood Mac (Special thanks to L. Buckingham) / Richard Dashut / Ken Caillat

Tracks: Not That Funny / Save Me A Place

THINK ABOUT ME

U.S. Release Date: March 1980

Catalogue Number: Warner Brothers WBS 49196

U.K. Release Date: May 1980

Catalogue Number: Warner Brothers K 17614

Producer: Fleetwood Mac (Special thanks to L. Buckingham) / Richard Dashut / Ken Caillat

Tracks: U.S. Think About Me / Save Me A Place

U.K. Think About Me / Honey Hi

SISTERS OF THE MOON

U.S. Release Date: May 1980

Catalogue Number: Warner Brothers WBS 49500

U.K. Release Date: Not Released

Catalogue Number:

Producer: Fleetwood Mac (Special thanks to L. Buckingham) / Richard Dashut / Ken Caillat

Tracks: Sisters Of The Moon / Walk A Thin Line

THE FARMER'S DAUGHTER

U.S. Release Date: March 1981

Catalogue Number: Warner Brothers WB 49700

U.K. Release Date: February 1981

Catalogue Number: Warner Brothers K 17746

Producer: Fleetwood Mac / Richard Dashut / Ken Caillat

Tracks: U.S. The farmer's Daughter / Monday Morning (Live)

U.K. The Farmer's Daughter / Dreams (Live)

FIREFLIES

U S. Release Date: February 1981

Catalogue Number: Warner Brothers WBS 49660

U.K. Release Date: Not Released

Catalogue Number:

Producer: Fleetwood Mac / Richard Dashut / Ken Caillat

Tracks: Fireflies / Over My Head (Live)

HOLD ME

U.S. Release Date: June 1982

Catalogue Number: Warner Brothers WBS 29966

U.K. Release Date: July 1982

Catalogue Number: Warner Brothers K 17965

Producer: Lindsey Buckingham / Richard Dashut / Ken Caillat

Fleetwood Mac

Tracks: Hold Me / Eyes Of The World

GYPSY

U.S. Release Date. September 1982

Catalogue Number: Warner Brothers WBS 29918

U.K. Release Date: September 1982

Catalogue Number: Warner Brothers K 17997

Producer: Lindsey Buckingham / Richard Dashut / Ken Caillat

Fleetwood Mac

Tracks: Gypsy (Edit) / Cool Water

LOVE IN STORE

U.S. Release Date: November 1982

Catalogue Number: Warner Brothers WBS 29918

U.K. Release Date: Not Released

Catalogue Number:

Producer: Lindsey Buckingham / Richard Dashut / Ken Caillat

Fleetwood Mac

Tracks: Love In Store / Can't Go Back.

OH DIANE

U.S. Release Date: March 1983

Catalogue Number: Warner Brothers 7-29698

U.K. Release Date: December 1982

Catalogue Number: Warner Brothers FLEET 1

Producer: Lindsey Buckingham / Richard Dashut / Ken Caillat / Fleetwood Mac

Tracks: U.S. Oh Diane / That's Alright

U.K. Oh Diane / Only Over You

U.K. 7" single Limited Edition picture disk FLEET 1P Oh Diane / Only Over You

U.K. 12" single FLEET 1T Oh Diane / Only Over You

CAN'T GO BACK

U.S. Release Date: Not Released

Catalogue Number:

U.K. Release Date: April 1983

Catalogue Number: Warner Brothers W 9848

Producer: Lindsey Buckingham / Richard Dashut / Ken Caillat

Tracks: Can't Go Back / That's Alright

U.K. 12" single W 9848T Can't Go Back / Rhiannon / Tusk / Over And Over

BLUES JAM AT CHESS

Fleetwood Mac
Otis Spann
Willie Dixon
Shakey Horton
J. T. Brown
Guitar Buddy
Honey Boy Edwards
S. P. Leary

BLUE HORIZON

7-66227

Stereo
Can also be played on mono equipment. See note over.

BIG LOVE

U.S. Release Date: March 1987

Catalogue Number: Warner Brothers W 28398

U.K. Release Date: March 1987

Catalogue Number: Warner Brothers W 8398

Producer: Lindsey Buckingham / Richard Dashut

*Fleetwood Mac / Richard Dashut / Ken Caillat / Chris Morris

Tracks: Big Love / You And I, Part I

U.K. 7" single W 8398F Limited Edition double pack Big Love / You And I, Part I / *The Chain / *Go Your Own Way

U.S. 12" single 0-20683 Big Love (Extended mix) / Big Love (House On The Hill Dub) / Big Love (Piano Dub) / You And I, Part 1

SEVEN WONDERS

U.S. Release Date: June 1987

Catalogue Number: Warner Brothers 28317

U.K. Release Date: June 1987

Catalogue Number: Warner Brothers W 8317

Producer: Lindsey Buckingham / Richard Dashut

Tracks: Seven Wonders / Book Of Miracles

U.S. 12" single 20739 Seven Wonders (Extended) / Book Of Miracles / Seven Wonders (Dub)

U.K. 12" single W 8317T and U.K. 12" single Limited Edition picture disk W 8317TP (Tracks as U.S. 12" single)

LITTLE LIES

U.S. Release Date: August 1987

Catalogue Number: Warner Brothers 28291

U.K. Release Date: September 1987

Catalogue Number: Warner Brothers W 8291

Producer: Lindsey Buckingham / Richard Dashut

Tracks: Little Lies / Ricky

U.S. 12" single Little Lies (Extended) / Little Lies (Dub) / Ricky

U.K. 12" single W 8291 T Little Lies Extended) / Little Lies(Dub) / Ricky

U.K. 12" single Limited Edition picture disk W 8291TP Little Lies (Extended) / Little Lies / Dub) / Ricky

EVERYWHERE

U.S. Release Date: November 1987

Catalogue Number: Warner Brothers 28143

U.K. Release Date: March 1988

Catalogue Number: Warner Brothers W 8143

Producer: Lindsey Buckingham / Richard Dashut

*Fleetwood Mac / Keith Olsen

Tracks: Everywhere / When I See You Again

U.K. 12" single W8143T Everywhere (Extended) / Everywhere (LP) / Everywhere (Dub) / When I See You Again

U.K. CD single W 8 143CD Everywhere / When I See You Again / *Rhiannon / *Say You Love Me

U.S. Cassette single 4-28143 Everywhere / When I See You Again

FAMILY MAN

U.S. Release Date: March 1988

Catalogue Number: Warner Brothers 28114

U.K. Release Date: September 1987

Catalogue Number: Warner Brothers W 8114

Producer: Lindsey Buckingham / Richard Dashut

Tracks: U.S. Family Man / You And 1, Part 2

U.K. Family Man / Down Endless Street

U.K. 7" single W 8114B Limited Edition Box Family Man / You And I ,Part 1 includes 2 special prints

U S. 12" single 0- 2084 Family Man (Extended Vocal Remix) / Family Man (I'm A Jazz Man Dub Mix) / Family Man (Extended Guitar Remix) / Family party (Bonus Beats) / Down Endless Street

U.K. 12" single W 8114T Family Man (Extended Vocal Remix) / Family Party (Bonus Beats) / You And 1, Part 2

U.S. Cassette single 4-28114 Family Man / You And I, Part 2

ISN'T IT MIDNIGHT

U.S. Release Date: Not Released

Catalogue Number:

U.K. Release Date: June 1988

Catalogue Number: Warner Brothers W 7860

Producer: Lindsey Buckingham / Richard Dashut

*Fleetwood Mac / Keith Olsen

Lindsey Buckingham / Richard Dashut / Ken Caillat / Fleetwood Mac

Tracks: Isn't It Midnight / Mystified

U.K. 12" single W 786OT Isn't It Midnight / Mystified / *Say You Love Me / #Gypsy

U.K. CD single W 786OCD Isn't It Midnight / Mystified / *Say You Love Me / #Gypsy

AS LONG AS YOU FOLLOW

U.S. Release Date: November 1988

Catalogue Number. Warner Brothers 7-27644

U.K. Release Date: December 1988

Catalogue Number: Warner Brothers W 7644

Producer: Greg Ladanyi / Fleetwood Mac

*Fleetwood Mac

#Fleetwood Mac / Richard Dashut / Ken Caillat

Tracks: As Long As You Follow / *Oh Well-Live

U.K. 12" single W 7644T As Long As You Follow / Oh Well-Live / #Gold Dust Woman

U.S. CD single 2- 27644 As Long As You Follow / Oh Well - Live / U.K. CD single W 7644CD As Long As You Follow / Oh Well-Live / Gold Dust Woman

U.S. Cassette single 4- 27644 As Long As You Follow / Oh Well-Live

U.K. Cassette single W7644C As Long As You Follow / Oh Well-Live

HOLD ME

U.S. Release Date: Not Released

Catalogue Number:

U.K. Release Date: February 1989

Catalogue Number: Warner Brothers W 7528

Producer: Lindsey Buckingham / Richard Dashut / Ken Caillat

*Greg Ladanyi / Fleetwood Mac

#Fleetwood Mac / Dennis Mays

Tracks: Hold Me / *No Questions Asked

U.K. 12" single W 7528T Hold Me / *No Questions Asked / I Loved Another Woman- Live

U.K. CD single W 7528CD Hold Me / No Questions Asked / I Loved Another Woman- Live

SAVE ME

U.S. Release Date: March 1990

Catalogue Number: Warner Brothers 7-019866

U.K. Release Date: April 1980

Catalogue Number: Warner Brothers W 9866

Producer: Greg Ladanyi / Fleetwood Mac

*Fleetwood Mac / Dennis Mays

Tracks: Save Me / Another Woman- Live

U.K. 12 " single W 9866T Save Me / *Another Woman-Live / *Everywhere-Live

U.K. CD single W 9866CD Save Me / *Another Woman-Live / The Second Time

U.K. CD single W 9866CDX Limited Edition gatefold sleeve

Save Me / *Another Woman-Live / The Second Time

U.S. Cassette single 4-019866 Save Me / Save Me

U.K. Cassette single W 9866C Save Me / *Another Woman-Live

SKIES THE LIMIT

U.S. Release Date: July 1990

Catalogue Number. Warner Brothers 7- 019867

U.K. Release Date: November 1990

Catalogue Number: Warner Brothers W 9740

Producer: Greg Ladanyi / Fleetwood Mac

Tracks: Skies The Limit / The Second Time

U.K. 12" single W 9740 Skies The Limit /

U.K. CD single W 9740T Skies The Limit /

U.S. Cassette single 4-019867 Skies The Limit / The Second Time

U.K. Cassette single W 9740C Skies The Limit / The Second Time

IN THE BACK OF MY MIND

U.S. Release Date: Not Released

Catalogue Number:

U.K. Release Date: August 1990

Catalogue Number: Warner Brothers W 9739

Producer: Greg Ladanyi / Fleetwood Mac

*Fleetwood Mac / Dennis Mays

#Mick Fleetwood / Dennis Mays

Tracks: In The Back Of My Mind / #Lizard People

U.K. 12" single W9739T In The Back OF My Mind / *Little Lies-Live / *The Chain-Live

U.K. CD single W 9739CD In The Back OF My Mind / U.K. Cassingle W 9739C In The Back Of My Mind / Lizard People

HARD FEELINGS

U.S. Release Date: October 1990

Catalogue Number: Warner Brothers 4-19537

U.K. Release Date: Not Released

Catalogue Number:

Producer: Greg Ladanyi / Fleetwood Mac

Tracks: Hard Feelings / Freedom

U.S. Cassette single 4 - 19537

REISSUES

SINGLES

The Green Manalishi(With The Two Pronged Crown) / Oh Well

U.S. Reprise 1079 (1982) GRE 0108 (1973)

U.K. Reprise K 14174(1973)

Albatross / Need Your Love So Bad

U.S. Not Released

U.K. CBS 8306(1973) CBS 5957(1978) CBS

7066(1979)CBS 7066 (1978)

Old Gold OG 9955 (1990)

Black Magic Woman / Stop Messin'Round

U.S. Not Released

U.K. CBS 1722 (1973)

Man Of The World / 'B'side-Danny Kirwan

U.S. DJM DJM 1007 (1976)

U.K. DJM DJS 10620 (1975) Epic SEPC 6466

(1978)

Albatross / Black Magic Woman

U.S. Epic 11029 (1976)

U.K. Not Released

Man Of The World / 'B'side-Humble Pie

U.S. Not Released

U.K. Old Gold OG 9529 (1985)

Albatross / Man Of The World

U.S. Not Released

U.K. CBS A4578 (1984) CBS 6546137 (1989)

**Albatross / Man Of The World / Black
Magic Woman / Love That Burns**

U.S. Not Released

U.K. 12" single CBS 654613 6 (1989)

U.K. 12" slngle CBS 654613 8 (1989)

U.K. CD single CBS 654613 2 (1989)

Over My Head / Rhiannon

U.S. Reprise GRE 0119

U.K. Not Released

Dreams / Go Your Own Way

U.S. Warner Brothers GWB 0348

U.K. Not Released

Tusk / Sara

U.S. Warnar Brothers GWB 0388

U.K. Not Released

Gypsy / Hold Me

U.S. Warner Brothers GWB 0439

U.K. Not Released

Don't Stop / Silver Springs

U.S. Warner Brothers 7 21990

U.K. Not Released

You Make Loving Fun / Say You Love Me

U.S. Warner Brothers 7 21991

U.K. Not Released

Little Lies / Everywhere

U.S. Warner Brothers 7 21888

U. K. Not Released

Seven Wonders / Big Love

U.S. Warner Brothers 7-21943

U.K. Not Released

**Albatross / Black Magic Woman / Need
Your Love So Bad / I'd Rather Go Blind**

U.S. Not Released

U.K. CD slngle CBS Solid Gold (1991)

U.K. Cassette single CBS Solid Gold (1991)

VIDEOS

**FLEETWOOD MAC DOCUMENTARY AND
LIVE CONCERT**

U.S. WEA PEV 4022 (1981)

U.K. Warner Home Video PEV 4022 (1981)

Tracks: Slsters Of The Moon / Walk A Thln

Line / Angel / Save Me A Place / Tusk /

Songbird / The Chain / Go Your Own Way /

Never Make Me Cry / Sara / Think About Me /

Not That Funny

Note: Available on RCA Selectavision Video

Disc (1981)

IN CONCERT MIRAGE TOUR 1982

U.S. RCA COLUMBIA PICTURES HOME

VIDEO (1984)

U.K. RCA RVT 10134 (1984)

Tracks: The Chain / Gypsy / Love In Store /

Not That Funny / You Make Lovlng Fun / I'm

So Afrald / Blue Letter / Rhiannon / Tusk /

Eyes Of The World / Go Your Own Way / Sisters

Of The Moon / Songbird

Note: Available on RCA Video Disc 12139 (1982)

TANGO IN THE NIGHT

U.S. Warner Reprise 120809 (1988)

U.K. Warners Home Video 9381493 (1988)

Tracks: The Chain / Everywhere / Dreams /

Seven Wonders / Isn't It Midnight / World

Turning / Little Lies / Oh Well / Gold Dust

Woman / Another Woman / Stand Back /

Songbird / Don't Stop

PUBLICATIONS

FLEETWOOD MAC - RUMOURS N'FAX

By Roy Carr and Steve Clarke

U.S. Harmony Books (1978)

U.K. Harmony Books (1978)

**THE AUTHORISED HISTORY - FLEETWOOD
MAC**

By Samuel Graham

U.S. Warner Brothers Publications Inc. (1978)

U.K. Not Released

FLEETWOOD MAC

By Steve Clarke

U.S. Proteus Publishing Company Inc. (1984)

U.K. Proteus Books Limited (1984)

FLEETWOOD MAC - BEHIND THE MASKS

By Bob Brunning

U.S. New English Library (Imported) (1991)

U.K. New English Library (1991)

**STEVIE NICKS - EVERYTHING YOU WANT
TO KNOW ABOUT...**

U.S. Ballantlne 34532238-4-295 AM

Communications (1985)

U. K. Not Released

ROCK'N'ROLL CUISINE

By Robin Le Mesurier & Peggy Sue Honeyman

Scott

U.S.

U.K. Aurum Press Ltd. (1988)

Note: Christine McVie, John McVie, Mick

Fleetwood, and Stevie Nlcks give their

favourite recipes in support of Phoenix House

**FLEETWOOD - MY LIFE AND ADVENTURES
IN FLEETWOOD MAC**

By Mick Fleetwood with Stephen Davis

U.S. William Morrow and Company Inc. New

York (1990)

U.K. Sedwick and Jackson (1990)

BOB BRUNNING DISCOGRAPHY

BOB BRUNNING APPEARS ON

ALBUMS

**BRUNNING HALL SUNFLOWER BLUES
BAND**

BULLEN STREET BLUES

U.S. Not Released

U.K. Saga FID 2118 (1969)

**BRUNNING HALL SUNFLOWER BLUES
BAND**

TRACKSIDE BLUES

U.S. Not Released

U.K. Saga EROS 8132 (1969)

TRAMP

TRAMP

U.S. Not Released

U.K. Music Man 603 (1969)

**BRUNNING HALL SUNFLOWER BLUES
BAND**

I WISH YOU WOULD

U.S. Not Released

U.K. Saga 8150

FIVES COMPANY

THE BALLAD OF FRED THE PIXIE

U.S. Not Released

U.K. Saga FID 2151 (1970)

DAVE KEILY

DAVE KELLY

U.S. Not Released

U.K. Mercury 63 1000 1 (1970)

J B HUTTO

HIPSHAKIN'-LIVE IN LONDON

U.S. Not Released

U.K. Flywright LP 502 (1971)

EDDIE BURNS

BOTTLE UP AND GO

U.S. Not Released

U.K. Action ACMP 100 (1972)

THE ORIGINAL FLEETWOOD MAC

Stereo
CAN ALSO BE PLAYED
ON MONO EQUIPMENT

CBS

SBP234277

The original Fleetwood Mac, with from left to right, Peter Green, Jeremy Spencer, John McVie & Mick Fleetwood

JOHNNY MARS

BLUES FROM MARS

U.S. Not Released

U.K. Polydor 2460

JIMMY DAWKINS

TRANSATLANTIC 770

U.S. Excello 80245 (1972)

U.K. Polydor 2311252 (1972)

HOMESICK JAMES AND SNOOKY PRIOR

HOMESICI(JAMES AND SNOOKY PRIOR

U.S. R Released

U.K. Carolina C 1502 (1974)

TRAMP

PUT A RECORD ON

U.S. Not Released

U.K. Spark SRLP 112 (1974)

EDDIE TAYLOR

READY FOR EDDIE

U.S. Not Released

U.K. Big Bear 6 (1974)

BIG JOHN WRENCHER

BIG JOHN'S WRENCHER

U.S. Not Released

U.K. Transatlantic Bear 10 (1974)

HOMESICK JAMES

HOME SWEET HOMESICK JAMES

U.S. Not Released

U.K. Transatlantic Bear 10 (1975)

ERWIN HELFER

BOOGIE PIANO CHICAGO STYLE

U.S. Not Released

U.K. Transatlantic Bear 11 (1975)

DR ROSS

JIVIN THE BLUES

U.S. Not Released

U.K. Transatlantic Bear 14 (1976)

ERROL DIXON

LISTEN TO THE BLUES

U.S. Not Released

U.K. Bellaphone BCH 33018 (1979)

JIMMY ROGERS AND LEFT HAND FRANK

CHICAGO BLUES

U.S. Not Released

U.K. JSP 1008 (1979)

JIMMY ROGERS AND LEFT HAND FRANK

LIVE

U.S. Not Released

U.K. JSP 1043 (1979)

JIMMY ROGERS AND LEFT HAND FRANK

THE DIRTY DOZENS

U.S. Not Released

U.K. JSP 1090 (1979)

DE LUXE BLUES BAND

LIVE AT HALF MOON PUTNEY

U.S. Not Released

U.K. Virgin Hot 1 (1981)

DE LUXE BLUES BAND

A STREET CAR NAMED DE-LUXE

U.S. Not Released

U.K. Appaloosa AP 040 (1981)

DE LUXE BLUES BAND

URBAN DE LUXE

U.S. Not Released

U.K. Appaloosa AP 040 (1983)

DAVE PEABOOY AND BOB HALL

ROLLIN' AND SLIDIN'

U.S. Not Released

U.K. Appaloosa AP 044 (1985)

MEMPHIS SLIM

LIVE AT RONNIE SCOTT'S

U.S. Not Released

U.K. Hendering WHCD 002 (1986)

DE LUXE BLUES BAND

DE LUXE BLUES BAND

U.S. Not Released

U.K. Blue Horizon / Ace BLUH 004 (1988)

DE LUXE BLUES BAND

MOTORVATING

U.S. Not Released

U.K. Appaloosa 1220601 (1988)

COMPILATION AND REISSUE ALBUMS

BRUNNING HALL SUNFLOWER BLUES BAND

BRUNNING HALL SUNFLOWER BLUES BAND

U.S. Not Released

U.K.Gemini 2010 (1971)

AMERICAN BLUES LEGENDS 74

AMERICAN BLUES LEGENDS 74

U.S. Big Bear 150202 (1974)

U.K. Transatlantic Bear 1 (1974)

VARIOUS ARTISTS

BLUES ON TWO

U.S. Not Released

U.K. BBC Records REN 610 (1986)

Note: Features De Luxe Blues Band

SINGLES

SAVOY BROWN

Taste And Try, Before You Buy / Someday People

U.S. Not Released

U.K. Decca 12702 (1967)

PETER GREEN DISCOGRAPHY

PETER GREEN ALBUMS

THE END OF THE GAME

U.S. Release Date: April 1971

Catalogue Number: Reprise 6436

U.K. Release Date: November 1970

Catalogue Number: Reprise RSLP 9006

Producer: Peter Green

Tracks: Bottoms Up / Timeless Time / Descending Scale / Burnt Foot / Hidden Depth / The End Of The Game.

Reissue: U.K. Reprise K44106 (1972)

IN THE SKIES

U.S. Release Date: November 1979

Catalogue Numbar: Sail / PVK 0110

U.K. Release Date: May 1979

Catalogue Number: PVK PVLS 101

Producer: Peter Vernen-Kell

Tracks: In The Skies / Slabo Day / Fool No

More / Tribal Dance / Seven Stars / Funky Chunk / Just For You / Proud Pinto / The Apostle.

Note: U.K. Some copies green vinyl

LITTLE DREAMER

U.S. Release Date: September 1980

Catalogue Number: Sail / PVK 0112

U.K. Release Date: April 1980

Catalogue Number: PVK PVLS 102

Producer: Peter Vernon-Kell

Tracks: Loser Two Times / Mama Don'tcha Cry / Born Under A Bad Sign / I Could Not Ask For More / Baby When The Sun Goes Down / Walkin' The Road / One Woman Love / Cryin' Won't Bring You Back / Little Dreamer.

WATCHA GONNA DO

U.S. Release Date: Not Released

Catalogue Number:

U.K. Release Date:. March 1981

Catalogue Number: PVK PET 1

Producer: Peter Vernon-Kell

Tracks: Gotta See Her Tonight / Promised Land / Bullet In The Sky / Give Me Back My Freedom / Last Train To San Antone / To Break Your Heart / Bizzy Lizzy / Last My Love / Like A Hot Tomato / Head Against The Wall.

BLUE GUITAR

U.S. Release Date: Not Released

Cataloguee Number:

U.K. Release Date November 1981

Catalogue Number: Creole CRX 5

Producer: Peter Vernon-Kell

Tracks: Apostle / A Fool No More / Loser Two Times / Slabo Day / Cryin'Won't Bring You Back / Gotta See Her Tonight / Last Train To San Antone / Woman Don't / Watcha Gonna Do / Walkin' The Road.

Note: U.K. Some copies blue vinyl

WHITE SKY

U.S. Release Date: Not Released

Catalogue Number:

U.K. Release Date: June 1982

Catalogue Number: Headline HED 1

Producer: Peter Green / Geoff Robinson

Tracks: Time For Me To Go / Shining Star / The Clown / White Sky (Love That Evil Woman) / It's Gonna Be Me / Born On The Wild Side / Fallin' Apart / Indian Lover / Just Another Guy.

Fleetwood Mac

Future Games.

KOLORS

U.S. Release Date: Not Released

Catalogue Number:

U.K. Release Date: November 1983

Catalogue Number: Headline HED 2

Producer: Ron Lee

Tracks: What Am I Doing Here? / Bad Bad Feeling / Big Boy Now / Black Woman / Bandit / Same Old Blues / Liquor And You / Gotta Do It With Me / Funky Jam

COME ON DOWN

U.S. Release Date:. Not Released

Catalogue Number:

U.K. Release Date: February 1986

Catalogue Number: Homestead HMS 031

Producer:

Tracks:

U.K. CD Homestead

LEGEND

U.S. Release Date: Not Released

Catalogue Number:

U.K. Release Date: January 1988

Catalogue Number: Creole CRX 12

Producer: Not credited

Tracks: Touch My Spirit / Six String Guitar / Proud Pinto / The Clown / You Won't See Me Anymore / Long Way From Home / In Thev Skies / Rubbing My Eyes / What Am I Doing Here / Corner Of My Mind / Carry My Love / Bandit.

U K CD Creole has two additionial tracks, Ltttle Dreamer / White Sky.

BACKTRACKIN'

U.S. Release Date: Not Released

Catalogue Number:

U.K. Release Date: January 1990

Catalogue Number: Masterpiece 101M / S

Producer: Various

Tracks: In The Skies / Fool No More / Tribal Dance / Just For You / Born On The Wild Side / Proud Pinto / Shining Star / Slabo Day / Indian Lover / Carry My Love / Corner Of My Mind / Cryin'Won't Bring You Back / Little Dreamer / Momma Don'tcha Cry / Baby When The Sun Goes Down / Born Under A Bad Sign / Walkin' The Road / Loser Two Times / What Am I

Doing Here / Big Boy Now / Time For Me To Go / It's Gonna Be Me / You Won't See Me Anymore / Bad Bad Feeling.

U.K. CD Masterpiece TRKCD 101

PETER GREEN SINGLES

HEAVY HEART

U.S. Release Date: Not Released

Catalogue Number:

U.K. Release Date: June 1971

Catalogue Number: Reprise RS 27012

Producer: Peter Green

Tracks: Heart / No Way Out

Reissue U.K. Reprise K 14092

NIGEL WATSON and PETER GREEN

BEASTS OF BURDFN

U.S. Release Date: Not Released

Catalogue Number:

U.K. Release Date: July 1972

Catalogue Number: Reprise K 14141

Producer: No Credit

Tracks: Beasts Of Burden / Uganda Woman

THE APOSTLE

U.S. Release Date:

Catalogue Number:

U.K. Release Date: June 1978

Catalogue Number: PVK PV 16

Producer: Peter Vernon-Kell

Tracks: The Apostle / Tribal Dance

IN THE SKIES

U.S. Release Date:

Catalogue Number:

U.K. Release Date: July 1979

Catalogue Number: PVK PV24

Producer: Peter Vernon-Kell

Tracks: In The Skies / Proud Pinto

Note: U.K. Some copies green vinyl

WALKIN'THE ROAD

U.S. Release Date:

Catalogue Number:

U.K. Release Date: April 1980

Catalogue Number: PVK PV 36

Producer: Peter Vernon-Kell

Tracks: Walkin'The Road / Woman Don't

LOSER TWO TIMES

U.S. Release Date:

Catalogue Number:

U.K. Release Date: June 1980

Catalogue Number: PVK PV41

Producer: Peter Vernon-Kell

Tracks: Loser Two Times / Momma Don'tcha Cry

GIVE ME BACK MY FREEDOM

U.S. Release Date:

Catalogue Number:

U.K. Release Date: March 1981

Catalogue Number: PVK PV 103

Producer: Peter Vernon-Kell

Tracks: Give Me Back My Freedom / Lost My Love

PROMISED LAND

U.S. Release Date:

Catalogue Number:

U.K. Release Date: July 1981

Catalogue Number: PVK PV 112

Producer: Peter Vernon-Kell

Tracks: Promised Land / Bizzy Lizzy

THE CLOWN

U.S. Release Date:

Catalogue Number:

U.K. Release Date: June 1982

Catalogue Number: Headline LIN 2

Producer: Peter Green / Geoff Robinson

Tracks:. The Clown / Time For Me To Go

BIG BOY NOW

U.S. Release Date:.

Catalogue Number:

U.K. Release Date: 1983

Catalogue Number:

Producer: Ron Lee

Tracks:. Big Boy Now / Bandit

PETER GREEN APPEARS ON

ALBUMS

EDDIE BOYD

7936 SOUTH RHODES

U.S. Not Released

U.K. Blue Horizon 7-632O2 (1968)

DUSTER BENNETT

SMILING LIKE I'M HAPPY

U K Blue Horizon 7-63208 (1968)

GORDON SMITH

LONG OVERDUE

U.S. Not Released

U.K. Blue Horizon 7-63211 (1968)

JOHN MAYALL

BLUES FROM LAUREL CANYON

U.S. London PS 545 (1968)

U.K. Decca SKL 4972 (1968)

OTIS SPANN

THE BIGGEST THING SINCE COLOSSUS

U.S. Blue Horizon 4802 (1969)

U.K. Blue Horizon 7-63217 (1969)

BRUNNING HALL SUNFLOWER BLUES BAND

TRACKSI DE BLUES

U.S. Not Released

U.K. Saga EROS 8132 (1969)

DUSTER BENNETT

JUSTA DUSTER

U.S. Blue Horizon 4804 (1969)

U.K. Nol Released

JO ANN KELLY

JO ANN KELLY

U.S. Epic 26491 (1969)

U.K. CBS 63841 (1969)

JEREMY SPENCER

JEREMY SPENCER

U.S. Not Released

U.K. Reprise RSLP 9002 (1970)

BRUNNING HALL SUNFLOWER BLUES BAND

I WISH YOU WOULD

U.S. Not Released

U.K. Saga 8150 (1970)

DUSTER BENNETT

12 DB's

U.S. Blue Horizon 4812 (1970)

U.K. Blue Horizon 7-63868 (1970)

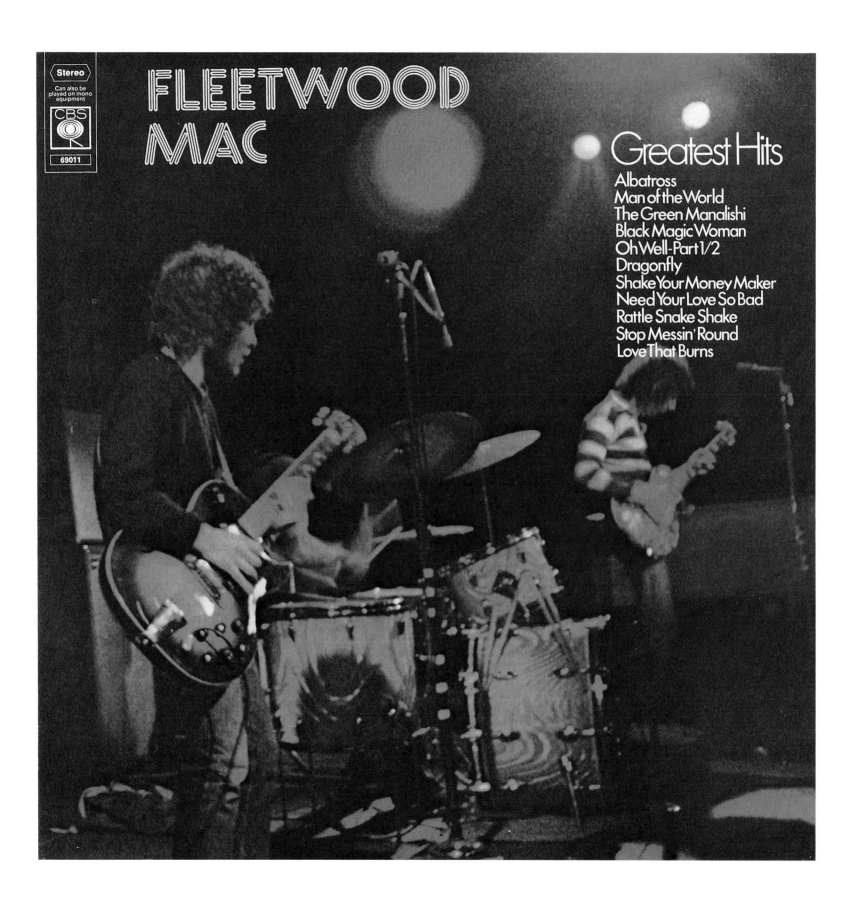

Stereo
Can also be played on mono equipment

CBS
69011

FLEETWOOD MAC

Greatest Hits

Albatross
Man of the World
The Green Manalishi
Black Magic Woman
Oh Well-Part 1/2
Dragonfly
Shake Your Money Maker
Need Your Love So Bad
Rattle Snake Shake
Stop Messin' Round
Love That Burns

DUSTER BENNETT

BRIGHT LIGHTS

U.S. Not Released

U.K. Blue Horizon 7-63221 (1970)

PETER BARDENS

THE ANSWER

U.S. Verve 3088 (1970)

U.K. Transatlantic TRA 222 (1970)

DAVE KELLY

DAVE KELLY

U.S. Not Released

U.K. Mercury 6310001 (1971)

MEMPHIS SLIM

BLUE MEMPHIS SUITE

U.S. Warner Brothers 1899 (1971)

U.K. Barkley G2024 (1971)

B.B. KING

B.B. KING-IN LONDON

U.S. ABC 730 (1971)

U.K. Probe SBP 1041 (1971)

FLEETWOOOD MAC

PENGUIN

U.S. Reprise MS 2138 (1973)

U.K. Reprise K44235 (1973)

THE TROGGS

THE TROGGS

U.S. Pye 12112 (1975)

U.K. Penny Farthing PEN 543 (1975)

PETER BARDENS

VINTAGE '69

U.S. Not Released

U.K. Transatlantic Transam 36 (1976)

FLEETWOOD MAC

TUSK

U.S. Warner Brothers 3350 (1979)

U.K. Warner Brothers K66088 (1979)

GASS

GASS

U.S. Not Released

U.K. Polydor 2383022 (1979)

MICK FLEETWOOD

THE VISITOR

U.S. RCA APL 14080 (1981)

U.K. RCA RCALP 5044 (1981)

BRIAN KNIGHT

A DARK HORSE

U.S. Not Released

U.K. PVK BRY1 (1981)

THE ENEMY WITHIN

A TOUCH OF SUNBURN

U.S. Not Released

U.K. Raven RL 0067 (1986)

KATMANDU

A CASE FOR THE BLUES

U.S. Not Released

U.K. Nightflite NTFL2001 (1986)

NOTE: Released on CD only as-

**GREEN, PETER, MIKE GREEN & THE
ENEMY WITHIN**

TWO GREENS MAKE A BLUES

U.S. Not Released

U.K. Red Lightning Records RLCD 0087 (1991)

NOTE: Includes 3 additional tracks

SINGLES

EDDIE BOYD

The Big Boat / Sent For You Yesterday

U.S. Not Released

U.K. Blue Horizon 57-3137 (1968)

DUSTER BENNETT

It's A Man Down There / Things Are Changeing

U.S. Not Released

U.K. Blue Horizon 57-3 141 (1968)

JOHN MAYALL

Jenny / Picture On The Wall

U.S.

U.K. Decca SKL 4972 (1968)

OTIS SPANN

Walkin' / Temperature Is Rising(98.8F)

U.S. Not Released

U.K. Blue Horizon 57-3 155 (1969)

OTIS SPANN

Hungry Country Girl / Walkin'

U.S. Blue Horizon 304 (1969)

U.K. Not Released

CLIFFORD DAVIS

Before The Beginning / Man Of The World

U.S. Not Released

U.K. Reprise RS 27003 (1969)

CLIFFORD DAVIS

Come On Down And Follow Me / Homework

U.S. Not Released

U.K. Reprise 27008 (1970)

CLIFFORD DAVIS

Man Of The World / Before The Beginning

U.S. Not Released

U.K. Reprlse K 14282 (1973)

JEREMY SPENCER DISCOGRAPHY

JEREMY SPENCER ALBUMS

JEREMY SPENCER

U.S. Release Date Not Released

Catalogue Number:

U.K. Release Date: January 1970

Catalogue Number: Reprise RSLP 9002

Producer: Jeremy Spencer

Tracks: Linda / The Shape I'm I n / Mean Blues
/ String-A-Long / Here Comes Charlie (With His
Dancing Shoes On) / Teenage Love Affair /
Jenny Lee / Don't Go,Please Stay / You Made A
Hit / Take A Look Around Mrs. Brown / Surfin
Girl / If I Could Swim The Mountain.

JEREMY SPENCER AND THE CHILDREN

U.S. Release Date: November 1972

Catalogue Number: Columbia KC 31990

U.K. Release Date: September 1973

Catalogue Number: CBS 69046

Producer: Jeremy Spencer

Tracks: Can You Here The Song / The World In
Her Heart / Joan Of Arc / The Prophet / When I
Look To See The Mountains / Let's Get On
The Ball / Someone Told Me / Beauty For Ashes /
War Horse / I Believe In Jesus.

FLEE

U.S. Release Date June 1979

Catalogue Number: Atlantic 19236

U.K. Release Date: October 1979

Catalogue Number: Atlantic K 50624

Producer: Jeremy Spencer / Michael Fogarty

Tracks: Deeper / Sunshine / Love Our Way Out
Of Here / Flee / Cool Breeze / You've Got The
Right / Travellin'.

JEREMY SPENCER SINGLES

LINDA

U.S. Release Date: Not Released

Catalogue Number:

U.K. Release Date: November 1969

Catalogue Number: Reprise RS 27002

Tracks: Linda / Teenage Darling

COOL BREEZE

U.S. Release Date: June 1979

Catalogue Number: Atlantic 3588

U.K. Release Date: August 1979

Catalogue Number: Atlantic K 11363

Producer: Jeremy Spencer / Michael Fogarty

Tracks: Cool Breeze / Travellin'

JEREMY SPENCER APPEARS ON

SINGLES

CLIFFORD DAVIS

Before The Beginning / Man Of The World

U.S. Not Released

U.K. Reprise RS 27003 (1969)

CLIFFORD DAVIS

Come On Down And Follow Me / Homework

U.S. Not Released

U.K. Reprise 27008 (1970)

CLIFFORD DAVIS

Man Of The World / Before The Beginning

U.S. Not Released

U.K. Reprise K 14282 (1973)

DANNY KIRWAN DISCOGRAPHY

DANNY KIRWAN ALBUMS

SECOND CHAPTER

U.S. Release Date: November 1975

Catalogue Number: DJM DJMJLPA 1

U.K. Release Date: September 1975

Catalogue Number: DJM DJLPS 454

Producer: Martin Rushent

Tracks: Ram Jam City / Odds And Ends / Hot Summer's Day / Mary Jane / Skip A Dee Doo / Love Can Always Bring You Happiness / Second Chapter / Lovely Days / Falling In Love With You / Silver Streams / Best Girl in The World / Cascades.

Reissue: U.K. DJM DJF 20454

MIDNIGHT IN SAN JUAN

U.S. Release Date: May 1977

Catalogue Number: DJM DJLPA 9

U.K. Release Date: September 1976

Catalogue Number: DJM DJF 20481

Producer: Clifford Davis Productions Ltd.

Tracks: I Can Tell / Life Machine / Midnight In San Juan / Let It Be / Angel's Delight / Windy Autumn Day / Misty River / Rolling Hills / I Can't Let You Go / Look Around You / Castaway.

HELLO THERE BIG BOY

U.S. Release Date: March 1979

Catalogue Number: DJM DJM 22

U.K. Release Date: March 1979

Catalogue Number: DJM DJF 20555

Producer: Clifford Davis

Tracks: Wings Of A Dove / Gettin'The Feeling / End Up Crying / Caroline / Only You / California / Space Man / Su mmer Days And Summer Nlghts.

DANNY KIRWAN SINGLES

RAM JAM CI TY

U.S. Release Date: Not Released

Catalogue Number:

U.K. Release Date: July 1975

Catalogue Number: DJM DJS10709

Producer: Clifford Davis Productions

Tracks: Ram Jam City / Angel's Delight

RAM JAM CITY

U.S. Release Date: November 1975

Catalogue Number: DJM DJUS 1004

U.K. Release Date: July 1975

Catalogue Number: DJM DJS 396

Producer: Clifford Davis Productions

Tracks: Ram Jam City / Hot Summer's Day

MISTY RIVER

U.S. Release Date: Not Released

Catalogue Number:

U.K. Release Date: May 1976

Catalogue Number: DJM DJS 666

Producer: Clifford Davis Productions

Tracks: Misty River / Rolling Hills

SECOND CHAPTER

U.S. Release Date: August 1976

Catalogue Number DJM DJUS 1014

U.K. Release Date: Not Released

Catalogue Number:

Producer: Martin Rushent

Tracks: Second Chapter / Skip A Dee Doo

Note: Promo only copies pressed

HOT SUMMER'S DAY

U.S. Release Date: Not Released

Catalogue Number:

U.K. Release Date: June 1977

Catalogue Number: DJM DJS 10783

P roducer: Martin Rushent

Tracks: Hot Summer's Day / Love Can Always Bring You Happiness

LET IT BE

U.S. Release Date: August 1977

Catalogue Number: DJM DJUS 1025

U.K. Release Date: Not Released

Calalogue Number:

Producer: Clifford Davis Productions

Tracks: Let It Be / I Can Tell

ONLY YOU

U.S. Release Date: Not Released

Catalogue Number:

U.K. Release Date: March 1979

Catalogue Number: DJM DJS 10896

Producer: CIifford Davis Productions Ltd.

Tracks: Only You / Caroline

DANNY KIRWAN APPEARS ON

ALBUMS

OTIS SPANN

THE BIGGEST THING SINCE COLOSSUS

U.S. Blue Horizon 4802 (1969)

U.K. Blue Horizon 7-63217 (1969)

TRAMP

TRAMP

U.S. Not Released

U.K. Music Man 603 (1970)

JEREMY SPENCER

JEREMY SPENCER

U.S. Not Released

U.K. Reprise RSLP 9002 (1970)

CHRISTINE PERFECT

CHRISTINE PERFECT

U.S. Not Released

U.K. Blue Horizon 7-63860 (1970)

CHRIS YOULDEN

NOWHERE CITY

U.S. London 663 (1973)

U.K. Detam SML 1009 (1973)

TRAMP

PUT A RECORD ON

U.S. Not Released

U.K. Spark SRLP 112 (1974)

SINGLES

OTIS SPANN

Walkin' / Temperature Is Rising (98.8F)

U.S. Not Released

U.K. Blue Horizon 57-3155 (1969)

OTIS SPANN

Hungry Country Girl / Walkin'

U.S. Blue Horizon 304 (1969)

U.K. Not Released

CHRISTINE PERFECT

When You Say / No Road Is The Right Road

U.S. Not Released

U.K. Blue Horizon 57-3165 (1969)

CLIFFORD DAVIS

Before The Beginning / Man 0f The World

U.S. Not Released

U.K. Reprise RS 27003 (1969)

JEREMY SPENCER

Linda / Teenage Darling

U.S. Not Released

U.K. Reprise RS 27002 (1969)

CLIFFORD DAVIS

Come On Down And Follow Me / Homework

U.S. Not Released

U.K. Reprise 27008 (1970)

CLIFFORD DAVIS

Man Of The World / Before The Beginning

U.S. Not Released

U.K. Reprlse K 14282 (1973)

REISSUE ALBUM

DANNY KIRWAN

DANNY KIRWAN

U.S. DJM DJM 9 (1981)

U.K. Not Released

REISSUE SINGLES

FLEETWOOD MAC

Man Of The World (A side)

DANNY KIRWAN

Second Chapter (B side)

U.S. Not Released

U.K. DJM DJS 10620 (1975)

FLEETWOOD MAC

Man Of The World (A side)

DANNY KIRWAN

Best Girl In The World (B side)

U.S. DJM DJM 1007 (1976)

U.K. Not Released

DAVE WALKER DISCOGRAPHY PRIOR TO JOINING FLEETWOOD MAC

DAVE WALKER APPEARS ON

ALBUMS

IDLE RACE

TIME IS

U.S. Not Released

U.K. Regal Zonophone SLRZ 1017 (1971)

SAVOY BROWN

STREET CORNER

U.S. Parrot 71047 (1971)

U.K. Decca TXS 104 (1971)

SAVOY BROWN

HELLBOUND TRAIL

U.S. Parrot 71024 (1972)

U.K. Decca TXS 107 (1972)

SAVOY BROWN

LIONS SHARE

U.S. Parrot 71057 (1973)

U.K. Decca SKL 5152 (1973)

DAVE WALKER DISCOGRAPHY

DAVE WALKER APPEARS ON

ALBUMS

MISTRESS

MISTRESS

U.S. RSO 13059 (1979)

U.K. RSO RSS14 (1979)

RAVEN

JOHN CIPOLLINAS RAVEN

U.S. line (Holland Import) 5041 (1980)

U.K. Line (Holland Import) 5041 (1980)

**BOB WESTON DISCOGRAPHY PRIOR TO
JOINING FLEETWOOD MAC**

BOB WESTON APPEARS ON

ALBUMS

BLACK CAT BONES

BARBED WIRE SANDWICH

U.S. Not Released

U.K. Nova SDN 15 (1970)

ASHKAN

IN FROM THE COLD

U.S. Sire 97017 (1970)

U.K. Nova SRN 1 (1970)

GRAHAM BOND

BOND IN AMERICA

U.S. Phillips 6499 200 (1971)

U.K. Mercury 6499 200 (1971)

ASHMAN REYNOLDS

STOP OFF

U.S. Polydor 5507 (1972)

U.K. Polydor 2383114 (1972)

BOB WESTON DISCOGRAPHY

BOB WESTON APPEARS ON

ALBUMS

DANA GILLESPIE

AIN'T GONNA PLAY NO SECOND FIDDLE

U.S. RCA APLI 0682 (1974)

U.K. RCA Victor APLI 0682 (1974)(Import)

HOWARD WERTH AND THE MOONBEAMS

KING BRILLIANT

U.S. Not Released

U.K. Charisma CAS 11004 & Rocket 2180 (1975)

MURRAY HEAD

SAY IT AIN'T SO

U.S. A & M 4558 (1975)

U.K. Island ISLP 9347 (1975)

ADRIAN WAGNER

INSTINCTS

U.S. Not Released

U.K. Charisma CAS 1124 (1977)

SANDY DENNY

RENDEZVOUS

U.S. Island 9433 (1977)

U.K. Island ISLP 9433 (1977)

DANNY KIRWAN

HELLO THERE BIG BOY

U.S. DJM DJM 22 (1979)

U.K. DJM DJF 20555 (1979)

MARK ASHTON

SOLO

U.S. Artista 5023 (1979)

U.K. Ariola ARL 5023 (1979)

ROBBIE PATTON

DISTANT SHORES

U.S. Liberty LT 1107 (1981)

U.K. Not Released

MURRAY HEAD

BETWEEN US

U.S. Not Released

U.K. Phillips (French Import) I MS 9101725 (1985)

VIDEOS

BOB WESTON APPEARS ON

VIDEO / LASERDISK

BOB WELCH

BOB WELCH AND FRIENDS LIVE AT
THE ROXY

U.S. Select A Vision / RCA Records Laserdisk
(1982)

U.K. Not Released

**BOB WELCH DISCOGRAPHY PRIOR TO
JOINING FLEETWOOD MAC**

BOB WELCH APPEARS ON

ALBUMS

BOB WELCH WITH HEAD WEST

BOB WELCH WITH HEAD WEST

U.S. Disques Vogue VCM - 6042 (1970)

Canadian Import

U.K. Not Released

SINGLES

SEVEN SOULS

I'm No Stranger/

U.S. OKEH Records (1966)

U.K. Not Released

SEVEN SOULS

Got To Find A Way/

U.S. Venture Records 71128 (1966)

U.K. Not Released

THE RAINBOWS

Love Of The Common People/Broken Heart
Like Mine

U.S. Capitol 45-5919 (1966)

U.K. Not Released

WINSTON GREY

Cherokee Sun/

U.S.

U.K.

BOB WELCH DISCOGRAPHY

BOB WELCH ALBUMS

FRENCH KISS

U.S. Release Date: September 1977

Catalogue Number: Capitol EST 11663

U.K. Release Date: November 1977

Catalogue Number: Capitol CL 15951

Producer: John Carter

*Lindsey Buckingham and Christine McVie

Tracks: *Sentimental Lady / Easy To Fall / Hot
Love,Cold World / Mystery Train / Lose My Heart
/ Outskirts / Ebony Eyes / Lose Your / Carolene /
Dancin'Eyes / Danchiva / Lose Your Heart.

Note: U.S. Limited edition picture disk
available Capitol ST 11663

THREE HEARTS

U.S. Release Date: February 1979

Catalogue Number: Capitol SO 11907

U.K. Release Date: April 1979

Catalogue Number: Capitol EA-ST 11907

Producer: John Carter

Tracks: 3 Hearts / Oh Jenny / I Saw Here
Standing There / Here Comes The Night /
China / The Ghost Of Flight 401 / Precious
Love / Church / Come Softly To Me / Devil
Wind / Don't Wait Too Long / Little Star.

THE OTHER ONE

U.S. Release Date: November 1979

Catalogue Number: Capitol SW 12017

U.K. Release Date: January 1980

Catalogue Number. Capitol E-ST 12017

Producer: John Carter

Tracks: Rebel Rouser / Love Came 2 x / Watch
The Animals / Straight Up / Hideaway / Future
Games / Oneonone / Don't Let Me Fall /
Spanish Dancers / Old Man Of 17.

MAN OVERBOARD

U.S. Release Date: September 1980

Catalogue Number: Capitol S00 12107

U.K. Release Date: November 1980

Catalogue Number: Capitol 12107

Producer: John Carter

Tracks: Man Overboard / Justlne / NIghtmare /
B 666 / Don't Rush The Good Things / The Girl
Can't Stop / Jealous / Fate Decides / Reason /
Those Days Are Gone.

BOB WELCH

U.S. Release Date: October 1981

Catalogue Number: RCA 4107

U.K. Release Date: March 1982

Catalogue Number: RCA 6019

Producer: Michael Verdick

Tracks: Two To Do / Remember / Bend Me Shape Me / That's What We Said/ If You Think You Know How To Love Me / It's What You Don't Say / You Can't Do That / Secrets / Imaginary Fool / To My Heart again / Drive.

EYE CONTACT

U.S. Release Date: June 1983

Catalogue Number: RCA AFL 14659

U.K. Release Date:

Catalogue Number:

Producer: American Girls / S.O.S. / Bernadette / He's Really Got A Hold On Her / Don't Let Me Touch You / I'll Dance Alone / Fever / Stay / Love On The Line / Can't Hold Back Your Love.

THE BEST OF BOB WELCH

U.S. Release Date: December 1991

Calalogue Number: Rhino 70597

U.K. Release Date:

Catalogue Number:

Producer: Various

Tracks: Black Book(Paris) / Blg Towne 2061 (Paris) / Sentimental Lady / Hot Love, Cold World / Ebony Eyes / Precious Love / Church / The Ghost Of Flight 401 / Don't Wait Too Long / Future Games / B 666 / Don't Stop (Bob Welch & Avenue'M').

Note: U.S. CD Rhino R2 70597 has four additional tracks - Heart Of Stone(Paris) / Blue Robin(Paris) / Rebel Rouser / Man Overboard.

BOB WELCH SINGLES

SENTIMENTAL LADY

U.S. Release Date: October 1977

Catalogue Number: Capitol 4479

U.K. Release Date: February 1978

Catalogue Number: Capitol CI 15970

Producer: John Carter

*Lindsey Buckingham and Christine McUie

Tracks: *Sentimental lady / Hot love,Cold World

EBONY EYES

U.S. Release Date: February 1978

Catalogue Number. Capitol 4543

U.K. Release Date: November 1977

Catalogue Number: Capitol CL 15951

Producer: John Carter

Tracks: U.S. Ebony Eyes / Outskirts

U.K. Ebony Eyes / Dancin'Eyes

HOT LOUE, COLD WORLD

U.S. Release Date: June 1978

Catalogue Number: Capitol 4588

U.K. Release Date: Not Released

Catalogue Number:

Producer: John Carter

Tracks: Hot Love, Cold World / Danchiva

PRECIOUS LOVE

U.S. Release Date: February 1979

Catalogue Number: Capitol 4685

U.K. Release Date: March 1979

Catalogue Number: Capitol CL 16070

Producer: John Carter

Tracks: Precious love / Something Strong

CHURCH

U.S. Released Date: May 1979

Catalogue Number: Capitol P 4719

U.K. Release Date: June 1979

Catalogue Number: Capitol CL 16086

Producer: John Carter

Tracks: U.S. Church / Here Comes The Night

U.K. Church / Don't Wait Too Long

REBEL ROUSER

U.S. Release Date: December 1979

Catalogue Number: Capitol P 4790

U.K. Release Date: Not Released

Catalogue Number:

Producer: John Carter

Tracks: Rebel Rouser /

DON'T LET ME FALL

U.S. Release Date: February 1980

Catalogue Number: Capitol P 4833

U. K. Release Date:

Catalogue Number:

Producer: John Carter

Tracks: Don't Let Me Fall

DON'T RUSH THE GOOD THINGS

U.S. Release Date: September 1980

Catalogue Number: Capitol P 4926

U.K. Release Date:

Catalogue Number:

Producer: John Carter

Tracks: Don't Rush The Good Things /

THE GIRL'S CAN'T STOP

U.S. Release Date: November 1980

Catalogue Number: Capitol P 4954

U.K. Release Date:

Catalogue Number:

Producer: John Carter

Tracks: The Girl's Can't Stop

TWO TO DO

U.S. Release Date: November 1981

Catalogue Number: RCA 12356

U.K. Release Date: February 1982

Catalogue Number: RCA RCA 189

Producer: Michael Verdick

Tracks: Two To Do / Imaginary Fool

FEVER

U.S. Release Date:

Catalogue Number:

U.K. Release Date

Catalogue Number:

Producer:

Tracks:

I'LL DANCE ALONE

U.S. Release Date: November 1983

Catalogue Number: RCA PB 13669

U.K. Release Date:

Catalogue Number:

Producer: Jeffrey Baxter

Tracks: I'll Dance Alone/

BOB WELCH APPEARS ON

ALBUMS

PARIS

PARIS

U.S. Capitol EST 11464 (1976)

U.K. Capitol ST 11464 (1976)

PARIS

BIG TOWNE 2061

U.S. Capitol ST 11560 (1976)

U.K. Capitol EA-ST 11560 (1976)

BILL WYMAN

STONE ALONE

U.S. Rolling Stones COC 79103 (1976)

U.K. Rolling Stones COC 59105 (1976)

TURLEY RICHARDS

THERFU

U.S. AtlantiC 19260 (1980)

U.K. Not Released

ROBBIE PATTON

DISTANT SHORES

U.S. Liberly LT 1107 (1981)

U.K. Not Released

SPIRIT

SPIRIT OF 84

U.S. Mercury 818514 (1984)

U.K. Not Released

Note: Released in the U.K. as: -

SPIRIT

THE 13th DREAM

U.S. Not Released

U.K. Polygram 818514 (1984)

SINGLES

PARIS

Big Towne 2061 / Blue Robin

U.S. Capitol 4356 (1976)

U.K. Not Released

VIDEO / LASERDISK

BOB WELCH

BOB WELCH AND FRIENDS LIVE AT THE ROXY

U.S. Select a Vision / RCA RecordS Laserdisk (1982)

U.K. Not Released

LINDSEY BUCKINGHAM DISCOGRAPHY PRIOR TO JOINING FLEETWOOD MAC

LINDSEY BUCKINGHAM APPEARS ON

ALBUMS

LAMBERT & NUTTYCOMBE
AS YOU WILL
U.S. 20th Century 415 (1969)
U.K. Not Released

BUCKINGHAM NICKS
U.S. Release Date: June 1973
Catalogue Number: Polydor 5058
U.K. Release Date: February 1977
Catalogue Number: Polydor 2391093
Producer: Keith Olsen
Tracks: Crying In The Night / Stephanie /
Without A Leg To Stand On / Crystal / Long
Distance Winner / Don't Let Me Down Again.
Django / Races Are Run / Lola (My Love) /
Frozen Love.
Reissue: U.K. Polydor 2482 378 June 1981

SINGLES

BUCKINGHAM NICKS
DON'T LET ME DOWN AGAIN
U.S. Release Date: November 1973
Catalogue Number: Polydor PD 14209
U.K. Release Date: April 1974
Catalogue Number: Polydor 206607
Producer: Keith Olsen
Tracks: U.S. Don't Let Me Down Again / Races
Are Run
U.K. Don't Let Me Down Again / Crystal

CATHRYN DUFFY & THE ENEMIES LIST
Nixon's The One / Pre Empeachment Blues
U.S. Takoma T45001 (1974)
U.K. Not Released

BUCKINGHAM NICKS
CRYING IN THE NIGHT
U.S. Release Date: February 1974
Catalogue Number: Polydor PD 14229
U.K. Release Date: Not Released
Catalogue Number:
Producer: Keith Olsen
Tracks: Crying In The Night / Without A Leg
To Stand On

BUCKINGHAM NICKS
CRYING IN THE NIGHT
U.S. Release Date: June 1976
Catalogue Number: Polydor PD 14335
U.K. Release Date: Not Released
Catalogue Number:
Producer: Keith Olsen
Tracks: Crying In The Night / Stephanie

LINDSEY BUCKINGHAM DISCOGRAPHY

LINDSEY BUCKINGHAM ALBUMS

LAW AND ORDER
U.S. Release Date: October 1981
Catalogue Number: Asylum SE 561
U.K. Release Date: November 1981
Catalogue Number: Mercury 6302 167
Producer: Lindsey Buckingham / Richard Dashut
Tracks: Bwana / Trouble / Mary Lee Jones / I'll
Tell You Now / It Was I / September Song /
Shadow Of The West / That's How We Do It In
L.A. / Johnny Stew / Love From Here, Love
From There / A Satisfied Mind.
U.S. CD Warner Brothers 2- 561
U.K. CD Mercury 800045 2 (1983)

GO INSANE
U.S. Release Date: August 1984
Catalogue Number: Electra 60363
U.K. Release Date: September 1984
Catalogue Number: Mercury MERL 46
Producer: Lindsey Buckingham / Gordon Fordyce
Tracks: I Want You / Go Insane / Slow Dancing
/ I Must Go / Play In The Rain / Play In The
Rain(continued) / Loving Cup / Bang The Drum
/ D.W. Suite
U.S. CD Warner Brothers 6036-2
U.K. CD Mercury 822450-2 (1984)

OUT OF THE CRADLE
U.S. Release Date: June 1992
Catalogue Number: Reprise Records 9 26182
U.K. Release Date: June 1992
Catalogue Number: Mercury 512658
Producer: Lindsey Buckingham / Richard Dashut
Tracks: Instrumental Introduction To: / Don't
Look Down / Wrong / Countdown / All My
Sorrows / Soul Drifter / Instrumental
Introduction To: / This Is The Time / You Do

Or You Don't / Street Of Dreams / Spoken
Introduction To: / Surrender The Rain / Doing
What I Can / Turn It On /This Nearly Was Mine /
Say We'll Meet Again.
U.S. CD Reprise 26182 (1992)
U.K. CD Mercury 512658

LINDSEY BUCKINGHAM SINGLES

TROUBLE
U. S. Release Date: October 1981
Catalogue Number: Asylum 47223
U.K. Release Date: November 1981
Catalogue Number: Mercury MER 85
Producer: Lindsey Buckingham / Richard Dashut
Tracks: U.S. Trouble / Mary Lee Jones
U.K. Trouble / That's How We Do It In L.A.

THE VISITOR (BWANA)
U.S. Release Date: Not Released
Catalogue Number:
U.K. Release Date: March 1982
Catalogue Number: Mercury MER 96
Producer: Lindsey Buckingham / Richard Dashut
Tracks: Bwana / A Satisfied Mind

IT WAS I
U.S. Release Date: March 1982
Catalogue Number: Asylum 47408
U.K. Release Date: Not Released
Catalogue Number.
Producer: Lindsey Buckingham / Richard Dashut
Tracks: It Was I / Love From Here, Love From
There

MARY LEE JONES
U.S. Release Date: Not Released
Catalogue Number:
U.K. Release Date: May 1982
Catalogue Number: Mercury MER 102
Producer: Lindsey Buckingham / Richard Dashut
Tracks: Mary Lee Jones / September Song

HOLIDAY ROAD
U.S. Release Date: July 1983
Catalogue Number: Warner Brothers 7- 29570
U.K. Release Date: July 1983
Catalogue Number: Mercury MER 150
Producer: Steve Wax
*Lindsey Buckingham / Richard Dashut
Tracks: Holiday Road / *Mary Lee Jones

GO INSANE
U.S. Release Date: July 1984
Catalogue Number: Electra 7-69714
U.K. Release Date: August 1984
Catalogue Number: Mercury MER 168
Producer: Lindsey Buckingham / Gordon Fordyce
Tracks: Go Insane / Play In The Rain
U.K. 12" single Mercury MERX 168 Go Insane /
Play In The Rain

SLOW DANCING
U.S. Release Date: October 1984
Catalogue Number: Electra 7-69675
U.K. Release Date: October 1984
Catalogue Number: Mercury MER 176
Producer: Lindsey Buckingham / Gordon
Fordyce
Tracks: Slow Dancing / D.W. Suite

COUNTDOWN
U.S. Release Date: Not Released
Catalogue Number:
U.K. Release Date: June 1992
Catalogue Number: Mercury MER 371
Producer: Lindsey Buckingham / Richard
Dashut
Tracks: Countdown / This Nearly Was Mine

REISSUES

Trouble / It Was I
U.S. WEA 7-65998
U.K. Not Released

LINDSEY BUCKINGHAM APPEARS ON

ALBUMS

BARON STEWART
BARTERING
U.S. United Artists LA 419G (1975)
U.K. Not Released

JERRY RIOPELIE
TAKE A CHANCE
U.S. ABC 0886 (1975)
U. K. Not Released

WARREN ZEVON

WARREN ZEVON

U.S. Asylum 7E 1060 (1976)

U.K. Asylum K 63039 (1976)

WALTER EGAN

FUNDEMENTAL ROLE

U.S. CBS 34679 (1977)

U.K. Polydor 231061 4 (1977)

BOB WELCH

FRENCH KISS

U.S. Capitol EST 11663 (1977)

U.K. Capitol CL 15951 (1977)

LEO SAYER

LEO SAYER

U.S. Warner Brothers 3200 (1978)

U.K. Chrysalis CHR 1198 (1978)

WALTER EGAN

NOT SHY

U.S. Columbia JC 35077 (1978)

U.K. Polydor 2310609 (1978)

WALTER EGAN

HI FI

U.S. Columbia JC 35796 (1979)

U.K. Polydor 2310673 (1979)

DANNY DOUMA

NIGHT EYES

U.S. Warner Brothers 3326 (1979)

U.K. Not Released

JOHN STEWART

BOMBS AWAY DREAM BABIES

U.S. RSO RS 103051 (1979)

U.K. RSO 2394228 (1979)

ROB GRILL

UPROOTED

U.S. Mercury SRM 13798 (1979)

U.K. Mercury 9111055 (1979)

TURLEY RICHARDS

THERFU

U.S. Atlantic 19260 (1980)

U.K. Not Released

Note: Lindsey does not play on this record, but
did the cover artwork

MALIBOOZ RULE

MALIBOOZ RULE

U.S. Rhino 100 (1981)

U.K. Not Released

ROBBIE PATTON

DISTANT SHORES

U.S. Liberty LT 1007 (1981)

U.K. Not Released

LINDA RONSTADT

GET CLOSER

U.S. Asylum 60185 (1982)

U.K. Asylum 960185 1 (1982)

WARREN ZEVON

THE ENVOY

U.S. Asylum 60159 (1982)

U.K. Asylum K 52345 (1982)

NICK REYNOLDS & JOHN STEWART

REVENGE OF THE BUDGIE

U.S. Takoma TAK 7106 (1983)

U.K. Not Released

RANDY NEWMAN

TROUBLE IN PARIDISE

U.S. Warner Brothers 23755 (1983)

U.K. Warner Brothers W 3755 (1983)

MICK FLEETWOOD

I'M NOT ME

U.S. RCA 4652 (1983)

U.K. RCA PL 84652 (1983)

JOHN STEWART

BLONDES

U.S. AI legiance AV 43 1 (1983)

U.K. Not Released

CHRISTINE McVIE

CHRISTINE McVIE

U.S. Warner Brothers 25059 (1984)

U.K. Warner Brothers 925029 I (1984)

JOSIE COTTON

FROM THE HIP

U.S. Electra 603091 (1984)

U.K. Not Released

ERIC CLAPTON

BEHIND THE SUN

U.S. Warner Brothers 25166 (1985)

U.K. Duck 9251661 (1985)

DON HENLEY

BUILDING THE PERFECT BEAST

U.S. Geffen 24026 (1985)

U.K. Geffen GEF 25939 (1985)

KIM CARNES

BARKING AT AIRPLANES

U.S. EMI SO- 17159 (1985)

U.K.

JOHN STEWART

THE LAST CAMPAIGN

U.S. Homecoming Records HC 00300 (1985)

U.K.

ESPIONAGE

ESP

U.S. Electra 60400- 1 (1985)

U.K.

VARIOUS ARTISTS-USA FOR AFRICA

WE ARE THE WORLD

U.S. Columbia USA 40043 (1985)

U.K. CBS USAID I (1985)

BELINDA CARLISLE

BELINDA

U.S. I RS 5741 (1986)

U. K. I RS MIRF 1012 (1986)

Note: Lindsey co-wrote "Since You've Been Gone"

DREAM ACADEMY

REMEMBRANCE DAYS

U.S. Reprise 9- 25625 (1987)

U.K. Blanco Y Negro BYN 12 (1987)

SOUNDTRACKS

VARIOUS ARTISTS

NATIONAL LAMPOON'S VACATION

U.S. Warner Brothers (1983)

U.K. Warner Brothers (1983)

VARIOUS ARTISTS

BACK TO THE FUTURE

U.S. MCA MCA 6144 (1985)

U.K. MCA MCF 3285 (1986)

VARIOUS ARTISTS

A FINE MESS

U.S. Motown (1986)

U.K. Motown (1986)

SINGLES

WARREN ZEVON

Hasten Down THe Wind / Mohammid's Radio

U.S. Asylum K 5356 (1976)

U.K. Not Released

WARREN ZEVON

I'll Sleep When I'm Dead / Mohammid's Radio

U.S. Not Released

U.K. Asylum K 10360 (1976)

WALTER EGAN

Magnet And Steel / She's So Tough

U.S. Not Released

U.K. Polydor 2001807 (1977)

WALTER EGAN

Only The lucky / I'd Rather Have Fun

U.S. CBS 3 10531 (1977)

U.K. United Artists UP 36245 (1977)

WALTER EGAN

When I Get My Wheels / Waitin'

U.S. CBS 310591 (1977)

U.K. United Artists UP 36321 (1977)

BOB WELCH

Sentimental Lady / Hot love, Cold World

U.S. Capitol 4479 (1977)

U.K. Capitol CL 15970 (1978)

WALTER EGAN

Magnet And Steel / Only The Lucky

U.S. Columbia 3- 10719 (1978)

U. K. Not Released

WALTER EGAN

Sweet South Breeze / Tunnel O'Love

U.S. Not Released

U.K. Polydor 2001807 (1978)

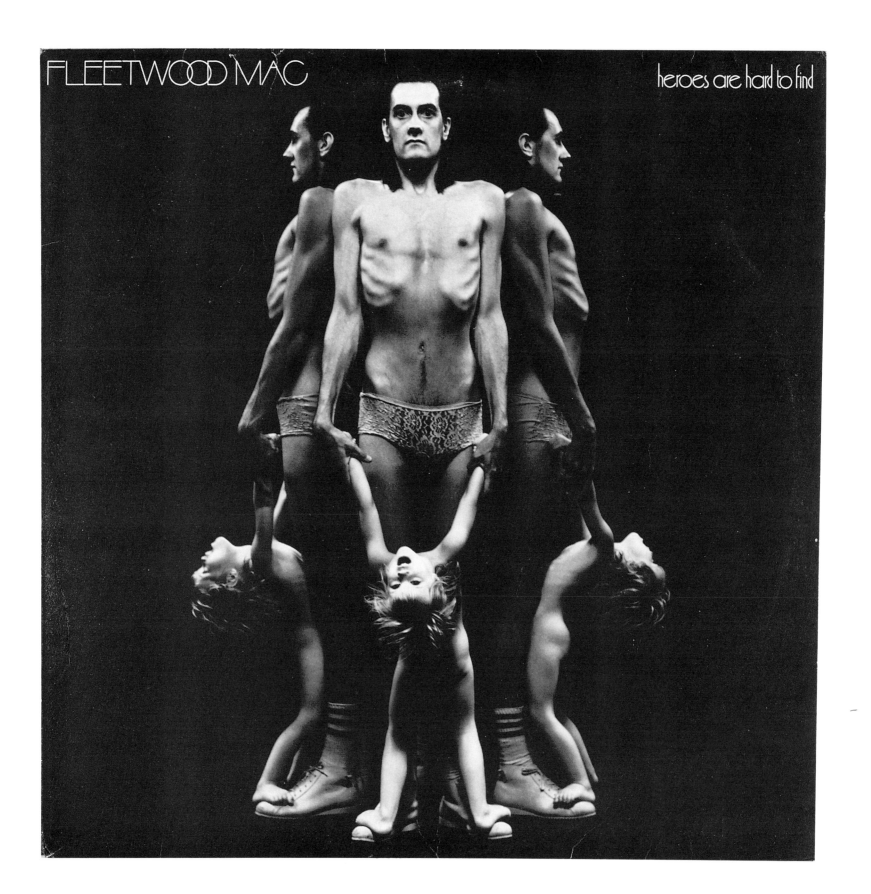

FLEETWOOD MAC

heroes are hard to find

WALTER EGAN

Hot Summer Nights / I'd Rather Have Fun

U.S. Columbia 310824 (1978)

U.K. Polydor 2001833 (1978)

LEO SAYER

Raining In My Heart /

U.S. Warner Brothers 8682 (1978)

U.K. Chrysalis CHS 2277 (1979)

WALTER EGAN

Unloved /

U.S. Columbia 310916 (1979)

U.K. Not Released

JOHN STEWART

Gold / Comin' Out Of Nowhere

U.S. RSO 931 (1979)

U.K. RSO 35 (1979)

JOHN STEWART

Midnight Wind / Comin' Out Of Nowhere

U.S. RSO 1000 (1979)

U.K. RSO 42 (1979)

JOHN STEWART

Runaway Fool Of Love / Heart Of The Dream

U.S. Not Released

U.K. RSO 51 (1979)

ROB GRILL

Rock Sugar / Have Mercy

U.S. Mercury 76009 (1979)

U.K. Mercury 6167 836 (1980)

RANDY NEWMAN

I Love L.A. / Song For The Dead

U.S. Warner Brothers 7-29687 (1983)

U.K. Warner Brothers 9687 (1983)

CHRISTINE McVIE

Got A Hold On Me / Who's Dreaming This
Dream

U.S. Warner Brothers 7- 29313 (1984)

U.K. Warner Brothers W 9372 (1984)

U.K. 12" single W 9372P Limited Edition
picture disk

CHRISTINE McVIE

Love Will Show Us How / The Challenge

U.S. Warner Brothers 7-29313 (1984)

U.K. Warner Brothers W 9313 (1984)

JOSIE COTTON

Jimmy Loves Maryann / No Pictures Of Dad

U.S. Electra E 9748 (1984)

U.K. Not Released

VARIOUS ARTISTS-USA FOR AFRICA

We Are The World / Grace

U.S. Columbia US7- 04839 (1985)

U.K. CBS USAID 1 (1985)

DREAM ACADEMY

Indian Summer / Heaven-Part 1

U.S. Warner Brothers 7-28199 (1987)

U.K. Blanco Y Negro NEG 27 (1987)

U.K. 12" single Blanco Y Negro NEG 27T
(1987)Indian Summer / Heaven-Part 1 / Indian
Summer

BRIAN WILSON

Love And Mercy / He Couldn't Get His Poor
Old Body To Move

U.S. Warner Brothers 7-27813 (1988)

U.K. Warner Brothers W 7814 (1988)

U.K. 12" single Warner Brothers W 7814T (1988)

U.K.5" CD single Warner Brothers W 7814CD
(1988)

VIDEOS

LINDSEY BUCKINGHAM APPEARS ON

VARIOUS ARTISTS- USA FOR AFRICA

WE ARE THE WORLD THE VIDEO EVENT

U.S. Music Vision 6-20475 (1985)

U.K. Not Released

**RICK VITO DISCOGRAPHY PRIOR TO
JOINING FLEETWOOD MAC**

RICK VITO APPEARS ON

ALBUMS

BOBBY WHITLOCK

RAW VELVET

U.S. Dunhill 50131 (1972)

U.K. CBS 65301 (1972)

TODD RUNDGREN

SOMETHING ANYTHING

U.S. Bearsville ZBX 2066 (1972)

U.K. Bearsville K 65501 (1972)

**SPANKY AND OUR GANG
CHANGE**

U.S. Epic 33580 (1975)

U.K. Not Released

JOHN PRINE

COMMON SENSE

U.S. AtlantiC S0 18127 (1975)

U.K. Atlantic K 50137 (1975)

JOHN MAYALL AND THE BLUESBREAKERS

NEW YEAR, NEW BAND, NEW COMPANY

U.S. ABC ABCD 6019 (1975)

U.K. ABC ABCL 5115 (1975)

JOHN MAYALL AND THE BLUESBREAKERS

NOTICE TO APPEAR

U.S. ABC ABCD 926 (1976)

U.K. ABC ABCL 5142 (1975)

JOHN MAYALL AND THE BLUESBREAKERS

BANQUET IN BLUES

U.S. ABC ABCD 958 (1976)

U.K. ABC ABCL 5187 (1976)

JOHN PRINE

PRIME PRINE

U.S. Atlantic SD 18202 (1976)

U.K. Not Released

ROGER McGUINN

THUNDERBYRDS

U.S. CBS 34656 (1977)

U.K. CBS 81883 (1977)

STEVE GOODMAN

HIGH AND OUTSIDE

U.S. Asylum 6E 174 (1979)

U.K. Asylum (1979)

JOHN MAYALL AND THE BLUESBREAKERS

NO MORE INTERVIEWS

U.S. DJM DJM 29 (1979)

U.K. DJM DJF 20564 (1979)

MARIA MULDAUR

OPEN YOUR EYES

U.S. Warner Brothers 3305 (1979)

U.K. Warner Brothers K 56634 (1979)

RONNIE BARRON

BLUE DELICACIES

U.S. Ace Records (1980)

U.K.

BONNIE RAITT

GREEN LIGHT

U.S. Warner Brothers BSK 3630 (1982)

U.K. Warner Brothers K 56980 (1982)

GREG COPELAND

REVENGE WILL COME

U.S. Geffen 2010 (1982)

U.K. Geffen GEF 85579 (1984)

JACKSON BROWNE

LAWYERS IN LOVE

U.S. Asylum 60268 (1983)

U.K. Asylum 9602681 (1983)

RITA COOLIDGE

INSIDE THE FIRE

U.S. A&M SP 5O03 (1984)

U.K. A&M AMA 5003 (1984)

JACKSON BROWNE

LIVES IN THE BALANCE

U.S. Asylum 60457 (1986)

U.K. Electra EKT 31 (1986)

BOB SEGER & THE SILVER BULLET BAND

LIKE A ROCK

U.S. Capitol 46195 (1986)

U.K. Capitol EST 2011 (1986)

VARIOUS ARTISTS

A VERY SPECIAL CHRISTMAS

U.S. A&M / SOL 3911 (1987)

U.K.

SINGLES

JACKSON BROWNE

Lawyers In Love / Say It Isn't True

U.S. Asylum 7-69826 (1983)

U.K. Electra E 9826 (1983)

FLEETWOOD MAC

JACKSON BROWNE

Tender Is The Night / On The Day

U.S. Asylum 7-69791 (1983)

U.K. Electra E 9791 (1983)

JACKSON BROWNE

In The Shape Of A Heart / Voice Of America

U.S. Asylum (1986)

U.K. Electra EKR 42 (1986)

BOB SEGER & THE SILVER BULLET BAND

Like A Rock(Edit) / Livin'Inside My Heart

U.S.

U.K. Capitol CL 408 (1986)

U.K. 12" single Capitol 12CL 408 Like A Rock
(Edit) / Livin' Inside My Heart / Katmandu

RICK VITO DISCOGRAPHY

RICK VITO ALBUMS

KING OF HEARTS

U.S. Release Date: February 1992

Catalogue Number: Modern Records 7 - 91789

U.K. Release Date: February 1992

Catalogue Number: WEA

Producer: Rick Vito / Lance Quinn / Terry Manning

Tracks: Walk Another Mile / I'll Never Leave
This Love Alive / Desiree / Honey Love / I Still
Have My Guitar / Pour Souls In Love / Knock
Me Down / Walking With The Deco Man /
Intuition / Two Hearts On Fire.

RICK VITO SINGLES

DESIREE

U.S. Release Date: February 1992

Catalogue Number: Modern Records

U.K. Release Date:

Catalogue Number:

Producer: Terry Manning / Rick Vito

Tracks: Desiree / Knock Me Down

RICK VITO APPEARS ON

ALBUMS

ROY ORBISON

MYSTERY GIRL

U.S. Virgin V2576 (1988)

U.K. Virgin 91058 (1988)

VARIOUS ARTISTS COMPILATION

ROCK, RHYTHM & BLUES

U.S. Warner Brothers 1 -25817 (1989)

U.K. WEA WX 225 (1989)

TROY NEWMAN

GYPSY MOON

U.S. East West America 91670 (1991)

U. K. Not Released

BOB SEGER

THE FIRE INSIDE

U.S. Capitol 91134 (1991)

U.K.

**BILLY BURNETTE DISCOGRAPHY PRIOR TO
JOINING FLEETWOOD MAC**

BILLY BURNETTE ALBUMS

BILLY BURNETTE

U.S. Release Date: May 1972

Catalogue Number: Entrance Z 31228

U.K. Release Date:

Catalogue Number:

Producer: Chips Moman * Reggie Young

Tracks: Always Wondering Bout You Babe
/*Going To A Party / Get On Down / Riff Raft
Man / Last War Song / Just My Love / To Bad I
Missed You / I Miss You Darling / I'm Getting
Wasted Doing Nothing / Twenty Years Ago, Today.

BILLY BURNETTE

U.S. Release Date: January 1979

Catalogue Number: Polydor 6187

U.K. Release Date:

Catalogue Number:

Producer: Chips Moman

Tracks: Shoo-Be-Doo / You Brought Me Back /
Niki Hoeky / Living Out Our Fantasies /
Walkin' Marsha Home / Believe What You Say /
I Ain't No Spaceman / Take a Listen-Llsten To
Your Heart / Dreamin' My Way Back To You /
Mississippi Line.

BETWEEN FRIENDS

U.S. Release Date: November 1979

Catalogue Number: Polydor PD 1 -6242

U.K. Release Date: November 1979

Catalogue Number: Polydor 2391436

Producer: Chips Moman

Tracks: What's A Little Love Between Friends /
All My Life / Are You Dreamin' The Same
Dream / Out-Run The Sun / Sittin'On The
Dock Of The Bay / Help Is On The Way / Hey,
You Got A Way / Love Is In Motion / Rain
Dance / Precious Time.

BILLY BURNETTE

U.S. Release Date: September 1980

Catalogue Number: Columbia JC 36792

U.K. Release Date:

Catalogue Number:

Producer: Barry Seidel

Tracks: In Just A Heartbeat / Oh, Susan /
Danger Zone / Don't Say No / Rockin'L.A. /
Honey Hush /·Rockin'With Somebody New /
One Night / Sittin'On Ready / Angeline /
Tear It Up.

GIMME YOU

U.S. Release Date: 1981

Catalogue Number: CBS 87460

U.K. Release Date:

Catalogue Number:

Producer: Barry Seidel / Barry Beckett

Tracks: Watcha Gonna Do When The Sun Goes
Down / Gettin'Back(To You And Me) / The
Bigger The Love / I Don't Know Why / Gimme
You / Love Ain't Easy / Let The New Love
Begin / I Don't Want To Know / Gone Again /
Take You Around The World (In My Arms).

TRY ME

U.S. Release Date: 1985

Catalogue Number: MCA / Curb MCA 5604

U.K. Release Date:

Catalogue Number.

Producer: Richard Podolor

Tracks: Try Me / Ain't It Just Like Love / It
Ain't Over / Guitar Bug / I'm Not Me / Roll
Over / Who's Using Your Heart Tonight /
Talkin' Love / The Letter / Rock And Roll Lullaby.

SOLDIER OF LOVE

U.S. Release Date: 1986

Catalogue Number: MCA 5768

U.K. Release Date:

Catalogue Number:

Producer: David Malloy

Tracks: Soldier Of Love / You Leave It Up To
Me / We'll Take It Day By Day / Lets Take A
Drive / Slave To Your Love / I've Just Seen a
Face / What A Perfect Way / Blonde Ambition /
Looks Like It's Gonna Rain Today / Little Bit
Of Them In Me.

BILLY BURNETTE SINGLES

YOUNG BILLY BEAU

HEY DADDY

U.S. Release Date:

Catalogue Number: Dot Records

U.K. Release Date: Not Released

Catalogue Number:

Producer:

Tracks: Hey Daddy / Santa's Coffee

BILLY BEAU

JUST BECAUSE WE'RE KIDS

U.S. Release Date:

Catalogue Number: A & M

U.K. Release Date: Not Released

Producer:

Tracks: Just Because We're Kids / Little Girl-
Big Love

FROG PRINCE

U.S. Release Date:

Catalogue Number: Warner Brothers 7327

U.K. Release Date: Not Released

Catalogue Number:

Producer: Dave Hassinger

Tracks: Frog Prince / One Extreme To The
Other

SHOO-BE-DOO

U.S. Release Date: 1979

Catalogue Number: Polydor 14530

U. K. Release Date:

Catalogue Number:

Producer: Chips Moman

Tracks: Shoo-Be Doo /

**WHAT'S A LITTLE LOVE BETWEEN
FRIENDS**

U.S. Release Date: 1979 .

Catalogue Number: Polydor 2024

U.K. Release Date: January 1980

Catalogue Number: Polydor POSP 95

Producer: Chips Moman

Tracks: What's A Little Love Between Friends / Precious

DON'T SAY NO

U.S. Release Date: October 1980

Catalogue Number: Columbia 1 - 11380

U.K. Release Date:

Catalogue Number:

Producer: Barry Seidel

Tracks: Don't Say No / Rockin' L.A.

OH SUSAN

U.S. Release Date:

Catalogue Number: Columbia 1 11432

U.K. Release Date:

Catalogue Number:

Producer: Barry Seidel

Tracks: Oh Susan /

IN JUST A HEARTBEAT

U.S. Release Date: Not Released

Catalogue Number:

U.K. Release Date: February 1981

Catalogue Number: CBS 9591

Producer: Barry Seidel

Tracks: In Just A Heartbeat / Rockin' L.A.

TEAR IT UP

U.S. Release Date:

Catalogue Number:

U.K. Release Date: June 1981

Catalogue Number: CBS A 1283

Producer: Barry Seidel

Tracks: Tear It Up / Oh Susan

BLOW OUT THE CANDLE

U.S. Release Date:

Catalogue Number: Columbia 1802527

U.K. Release Date:

Catalogue Number:

Producer: Barry Seidel / Barry Becket

Tracks: Blow Out The Candle / Let The New Love Begin

THE BIGGER THE LOVE (THE HARDER THE FALL)

U.S. Release Date: April 1982

Catalogue Number: Columbia 1802699

U.K. Release Oate:

Catalogue Number:

Producer: Barry Seidel / Barry Backet

Tracks: The Bigger The Love (The Harder The Fall)

WHO'S USING YOUR HEART TONIGHT

U.S. Release Date: October 1985

Catalogue Number: MCA 52710

U.K. Release Date:

Catalogue Number:

Producer: Richard Podolor

Tracks: Who's Using Your Heart Tonight /

TRY ME

U.S. Release Date:

Catalogue Number: MCA 52749

U.K. Release Date:

Catalogue Number:

Producer: Richard Podolor

Tracks: Try Me /

AIN'T IT JUST LIKE LOVE

U.S. Release Date: July 1985

Catalogue Number: MCA 52626

U.K. Release Date:

Catalogue Number:

Producer: Richard Podolor

Tracks: Ain't It Just Like Love / Guitar Bug

IT AIN'T OVER

U.S. Release Date: 1985

Catalogue Number: MCA 52710

U.K. Release Date:

Catalogue Number:

Producer: Richard Podolor

Tracks: It Ain't Over /

SOLDIER OF LOVE

U.S. Release Date:

Catalogue Number: MCA 58852

U.K. Release Date:

Catalogue Number:

Producer:

Tracks: Soldier Of Love / Guitar Bug

BILLY BURNETTE APPEARS ON

ALBUMS

BLUE JUG BAND

BLUE JUG

U.S. Capricorn CP 01 S8 (1975)

U.K. Not Released

TOWNES VAN ZANT

FLYIN' SHOES

U.S. Tomatoe Tom 7017 (1978)

U.K. Charly LIK 59 (1989)

ROCKY BURNETTE

SON OF ROCK AND ROLL

U.S. EMI 17033 (1979)

U.K. EMI EMI 3323 (1979)

MICK FLEETWOOD'S ZOO

I'M NOT ME

U.S. RCA 46S2 (1983)

U.K. RCA PL 846S2 (1983)

JIMMY BARNES

JIMMY BARNES

U.S. Geffen GHS 24089 (1985)

U.K.

TODD SHARP

WHO AM I

U.S. MCA 5579 (1986)

U.K. Not Released

SOUNDTRACK

VARIOUS ARTISTS

JUST ONE OF THE GUYS

U.S. ELK 60426

U.K.

VIDEOS

BILLY BURNETTE APPEARS ON

VARIOUS ARTISTS

A CELEBRATION FOR DORSEY BURNETTE

U.S.

U.K.

CHRISTINE McVIE

CHRISTINE McVIE-THE VIDEO ALBUM

U.S. Vestron Music MA 1013 (1984)

U.K. Vestron 21013 CHRMI (1984)

BILLY BURNETTE DISCOGRAPHY

BILLY BURNETTE SINGLES

NOTHIN' TO DO (AND ALL NIGHT TO DO IT)

U.S. Release Date: January 1992

Catalogue Number: Warner Brothers 19042

U.K. Release Date:

Catalogue Number:

Producer: David Malloy

Tracks: Nothin' To Do (And All Night To Do It)/ Can't Get Over You

BILLY BURNETTE APPEARS ON

ALBUMS

ROY ORBISON

U.S. Virgin V2576 (1988)

U. K.

VARIOUS ARTISTS

ROCK, RHYTHM & BLUES

U.S. Warner Brothers 1 -25817 (1989)

U.K. WEA WX 225 (1989)

TROY NEWMAN

GYPSY MOON

U.S. East West America 91670 (1991)

U.K. Not Released

JOHN McVIE'S " GOTTA BAND" WITH LOLA THOMAS

JOHN McVIE'S " GOTTA BAND" WITH LOLA THOMAS

U.S. Warner Brothers 26909 (1992)

U.K. WEA 26909 (1992)

SINGLES

TROY NEWMAN

Love Gets Rough / Gypsy Girl

U.S. East West Records 74- 98801 (1991)

U.K. Not Released

TROY NEWMAN

God Only Knows /

U.S. East West America (1991)

U.K. Not Released

THE ZOO

Shakin' The Cage / Forgive

U.S. Not Released

U.K. Not Released

Note: Australian release only Mushroom K 10370 (1991)

FLEETWOOD MAC

t u s k

STEVIE NICKS DISCOGRAPHY PRIOR TO JOINING FLEETWOOD MAC

STEVIE NICKS APPEARS ON

ALBUMS

BUCKINGHAM NICKS

U.S. Release Date: June 1973
Catalogue Number: Polydor 5058
U.K. Release Date: February 1977
Catalogue Number: Polydor 2391093
Producer: Keith Olsen
Tracks: Crying In The Night / Stephanie / Without A Leg To Stand On / Crystal / Long Distance Winner / Don't Let Me Down Again / Django / Races Are Run / Lola(My Love) / Frozen Love.
Reissue: U.K. Polydor 2482 378 June 1981

SINGLES

BUCKINGHAM NICKS

DON'T LET ME DOWN AGAIN
U.S. Release Date November 1973
Catalogue Number: Polydor PD 14209
U.K. Release Date: April 1974
Catalogue Number: Polydor 2066077
Producer: Keith Olsen
Tracks: U.S. Don't Let Me Down Again / Races Are Run
U.K. Don't Let Me Down Again / Crystal

BUCKINGHAM NICKS

CRYING IN THE NIGHT
U.S. Release Date: February 1974
Catalogue Number: Polydor PD 14229
U.K. Release Date: Not Released
Catalogue Number:
Producer: Keith Olsen
Tracks: Crying In The Night / Without A Leg To Stand On

BUCKINGHAM NICKS

CRYING IN THE NIGHT
U.S. Release Date: June 1976
Catalogue Number: Polydor PD 14335
U.K. Release Date: Not Released
Catalogue Number:
Producer: Keith Olsen
Tracks: Crying In The Night / Stephanie

STEVIE NICKS DISCOGRAPHY

STEVIE NICKS ALBUMS

BELLA DONNA

U.S. Release Date: July 1981
Catalogue Number: Modern MR 38139
U.K. Release Date: July 1981
Catalogue Number: WEA K 99169
Producer: Jimmy Iovine
Tracks: Bella Donna / Kind Of Woman Stop Draggin' My Heart Around / Think About It / After The Glitter Fades / Edge Of Seventeen / How Still My Love / Leather And Lace / Outside The Rain / The Highwayman.
Reissue: U.K. EMI EMC 3562 (1989)
Original Master Recording MFSL 1 - 121
U.S. CD Modern 38139-2 (1984)
U.K. CD WEA 299169 (1984)
Reissue: U.K. CD EMI CDEMC 3563 / 7930092 (1989)

THE WILD HEART

U.S. Release Date: June 1983
Catalogue Number: WEA 2500711
Producer: Jimmy Iovine
Tracks: Wild Heart / If Anyone Falls / Gate And Garden / Enchanted / Nightbird / Stand Back / I Will Run To You / Nothing Ever Changes / Sable On Blond / Beauty And The Beast.
Reissue: U.K. EMI EMC 3563 / 793009 1 (1989)
U.S. CD Modern 90084-2 (1984)
U.K. CD WEA 250071 -2 (1984)
Reissue: U.K. CD EMI CDEMC 3563 / 7930092 (1989)

ROCK A LITTLE

U.S. Release Date: November 1985
Catalogue Number. Modern 90479-1
U.K. Release Date: December 1985
Catalogue Number: Parlophone PCS 7300
Produced: Stevie Nicks / Rick Nowels / Jimmy Iovine
Tracks: I Can't Wait / Rock A Little(Go Ahead Lily) / Sister Honey / I Sing For The Things / Imperial Hotel / If I Were You / No Spoken Word / Has Anyone Ever Written Anything For You.
Reissue: U.K. Parlophone ATAK 123 (1989)
U.S. CD Modern 90479-2 (1985)
U.K. CD Parophone CDP 7462012 / CZ80 (1986)

THE OTHER SIDE OF THE MIRROR

U.S. Release Date: May 1989
Catalogue Number: Modern 91245 - 1
U.K. Release Date: May 1989
Catalogue Number: EMI EMD 1008
Producer: Rupert Hine
Tracks: Rooms On Fire / Long Way To Go / Two Kinds Of Love / Ooh My Love / Ghosts / Whole Lotta Trouble / Fire Burning / Cry Wolf / Alice / Juliet / Doing The Best That I Can(Escape From Berlin) / I Still Mis Someone (Blue Eyes).
U.K. Limited Edition EMI 1008 includes a free hologram
U.S. CD Modern 791245- 2 (1989)
U.K. CD EMI CDEMD 1008 / 7925422 (1989)

TIME SPACE: THE BEST OF STEVIE NICKS

U.S. Release Date: September 1991
Catalogue Number: Modern 91711 - 1
U.K. Release Date: September 1991
Catalogue Number: EMI EMD 1024
Producer: Various
Tracks: Sometimes It's A Bitch / Stop Draggin' My Heart Around / Whole Lotta Trouble / Talk To Me / Stand Back / Beauty And The Beast / If Anyone Falls / Rooms On Fire / Love's A Hard Game To Play / Edge Of Seventeen / Leather And Lace / I Can't Wait / Has Anyone Ever Written Anything For You.
U.S.CD Modern 91711-2 (1991)
U.K. CD EMI EMCD 1024 (1991)

STEVIE NICKS SINGLES

STOP DRAGGIN' MY HEART AROUND

U.S. Release Date: July 1981
Catalogue Number: Modern MR 7336
U.K. Release Date: August 1981
Catalogue Number: WEA K 79231
Producer: *Jimmy Iovine and Tom Petty / Jimmy Iovine
Tracks: *Stop Draggin' My Heart Around / Kind Of Woman

LEATHER AND LACE

U.S. Release Date: October l981
Catalogue Number: Modern MR 7341
U.K. Release Date: October 1981
Catalogue Number: WEA K 79265

Producer: Jimmy Iovine
Tracks: U.S. Leather And Lace / Bella Donna
U.K. Leather And Lace / Outside The Rain

EDGE OF SEVENTEEN

U.S. Release Date: February 1982
Catalogue Number: Modern MR 7401
U.K. Release Date: April 1982
Catalogue Number: WEA K 79264
Producer: Jimmy Iovine
Tracks: U.S. Edge Of Seventeen / Edge Of Seventeen (Live)
U.K. Edge Of Seventeen / Outside The Rain

AFTER THE GLITTER FADES

U.S. Release Date: May 1982
Catalogue Number: Modern MR 7504
U.K. Release Date: Not Released
Catalogue Number:
Producer: Jimmy Iovine
Tracks: After The Glitter Fades / Think About It

STAND BACK

U.S. Release Date: June 1983
Catalogue Number: Modern 99863
U.K. Release Date: August 1983
Catalogue Number: WEA U 9870
Producer: Jimmy Iovine
Tracks: Stand Back / Garbo
U.K. 12" single WEA U 9870T Stand Back / Garbo / Wild Heart.

IF ANYONE FALLS

U.S. Release Date: August 1983
Catalogue Number: Modern 99799
U.K. Release Date: November 1983
Catalogue Number. WEA X 9590
Producer: Jimmy Iovine
Tracks: U.S. Nightbird / Gate And Garden
U.K. Nightbird / Nothing Ever Changes

NIGHTBIRD

U.S. Release Date: December 1983
Catalogue Number: Modern 99799
U.K. Release Date: January 1984
Catalogue Number: WEA U 9690
Producer: Jimmy Iovine
Tracks: U.S. Nightbird / Gate And Garden
U.K. Nightbird / Nothing Ever Changes

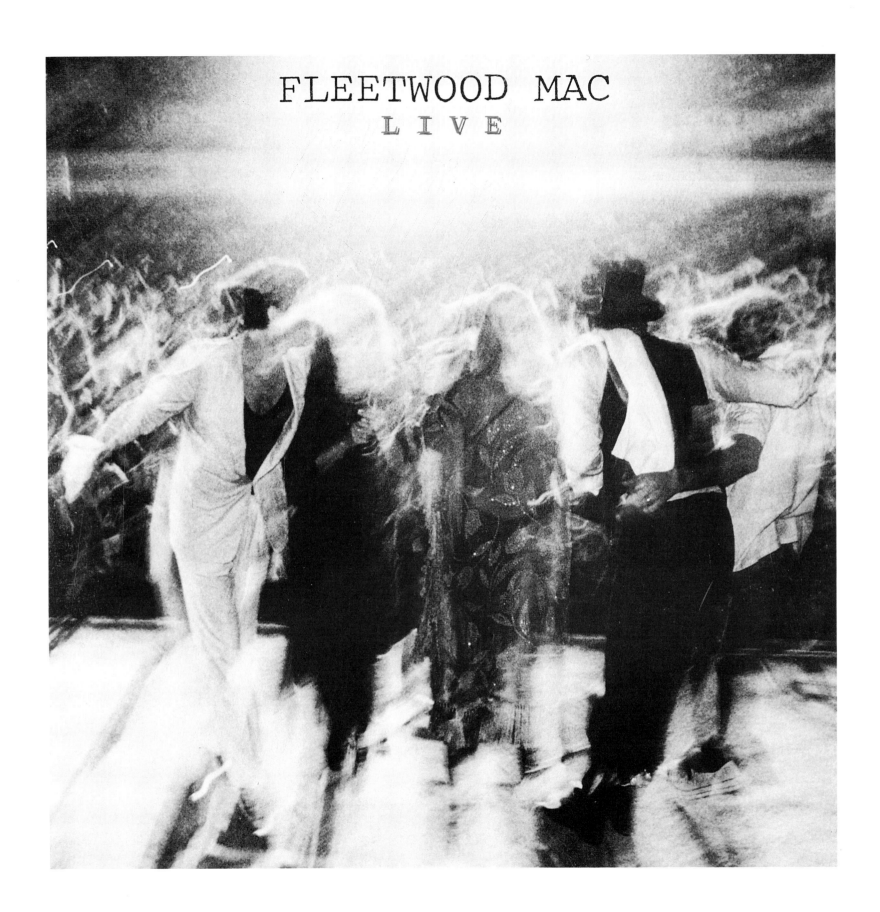

TALK TO ME

U.S. Release Date: November 1985
Catalogue Number: Modern 99582
U.K. Release Date: March 1986
Catalogue Number EMI R 6124
Producer: Jimmy Iovine / Chas Sandford
Tracks: Talk To Me / One More Big Time Rock And Roll Star.
U.K. 12" single EMI 12R 6124 Talk To Me / One More Big Time Rock and Roll Star / Imperial Hotel.

I CAN'T WAIT

U.S. Release Date: July 1986
Catalogue Number: Modern 99565
U.K. Release Date: January 1986
Catalogue Number: EMI R 6110
Producer: Rick Nowels / Jimmy Iovine
Tracks: U.S. I Can't Wait / The Nightmare
U.K. I Can't Wait / Rock A Little
U.S. 12" single Modern 0-968251 Can't Wait (Extended,Rock
and Dub mixes) / The Nightmare (Extended)
U.K. 12" single EM 1 12 R 6110 I Can't Wait (Extended) / Rock A Little / I Can't Wait

HAS ANYONE EVER WRITTEN ANYTHING FOR YOU

U.S. Release Date: May 1986
Catalogue Number: Modern 7- 99532
U.K. Release Date: August 1986
Catalogue Number: EMI 5574
Producer: Rick Nowels
Tracks: U.S. Has Anyone Ever Written Anything For You / Imperial Hotel
U.K. Has Anyone Ever Written Anything For You
U.K. 12" single 12EMI 5574 Has Anyone Ever Written
Anything For You / I Can't Wait / No Spoken Word

ROOMS ON FIRE

U.S. Release Date April 1989
Catalogue Number: Modern 7-99216
U.K. Release Date: April 1989
Catalogue Number: EMI EM 90
Producer: Rupert Hine
Tracks: Rooms On Fire / Alice
U.K. 12" single EMI 12 EM 90 Rooms On Fire / Alice / Has Anyone Ever Written Anything For You (Live)

U.K. 12" single Limited Edition EMI 12 Em 90 includes poster bag sleeve
U.K. CD single EMI CD EM 90 Rooms On Fire / Alice / Has Anyone Ever Written Anything For You (Live)
U.S. Cassette single Modern 74 - 99216 Rooms On Fire / Alice
U.K. Cassette single EMI TC EM 90 Rooms On Fire / Alice / Has Anyone Ever Written Anything For You (Live)

TWO KINDS OF LOVE

U.S. Release Date:
Catalogue Number: Modern 7- 99179
U.K. Release Date: Not Released
Catalogue Number:
Producer: Rupert Hine
Tracks: Two Kinds Of Love / Real Tears
U.S. Cassette single Modern 99179 Two Kinds Of Love / Two Kinds Of Love

LONG WAY TO GO

U.S. Release Date: Not Released
Catalogue Number:
U.K. Release Date: July 1989
Catalogue Number: EMI EM 97 / 2034317
Producer: Rupert Hine
Tracks: Long Way To Go / Real Tears
U.K. 12 " Single EM 112 EM 97 / 2034316 Long Way To Go (Remlx) / Long Way To Go(7" single version) / Real Tears
U.K. 12" single Limited Edition EMI 12 EM 97 / 2034318
includes gatefold sleeve
U.K. CD single EMI CD EM 97 / 20343 12 Long Way To Go
(7" single version) / Real Tears / No Spoken Word / Long Way To Go (Remix)
U.K. Cassette single EMI TC EM 97 / 2034314 Long Way To Go / Real Tears

WHOLE LOTTA TROUBLE

U.S. Release Date: Not Released
Catalogue Number:
U.K. Release Date: October 1989
Catalogue Number: EMI EM 114 / 2035837
Producer: Rupert Hine
Tracks: Whole Lotta Trouble / Edge Of Seventeen

U.K. 12" single EMI 12 EM 114 / 2035836
Whole Lotta Trouble / Edge Of Seventeen / Beauty And The Beast (Live)
U.K. 12" single Limited Edition EMI 12 EMP 114 / 2035830
includes a poster
U.K. CD single EMI CDEM 114 / 22035832
Whole Lotta Trouble / Beauty And The Beast (Live) / Rooms On Fire
U.S. Cassette single EMI TCEM 114 / 2035834
Whole Lotta Trouble / Edge Of Seventeen

SOMETIMES (IT'S A BITCH)

U.S. Release Date: August 1991
Catalogue Number:
U.K. Release Date: August 1991
Catalogue Number: EMI EM 203
Producer: Danny Korchmar / Jon Bon Jovi
*Stevie Nicks / Chris Lord-Alge / Michael Cambell
Tracks: Sometimes It's A Bitch / *Desert Angel
U.K. 7" single EMI EM 203 Limited Edition postcard pack
U.K. CD single EMI CDEM 203 Sometimes It's A Bitch / Battle Of The Dragons / Desert Angel

I CAN'T WAIT

U.S. Release Date: Not Released
Catalogue Number:
U.K. Release Date: November 1991
Catalogue Number: EMI EM 214
Producer. Rick Nowels / Jimmy Iovine
*Jimmy Iovine
Tracks: I Can't Wait / Sleeping Angel
U.K. 12" single EMI 12 EM S 214 I Can't Wait (Timespace and Dub Versions) / Sleeplng Angel
U.K. CD single EMI 12 CDEM 214 I Can't Wait (Timespace and Dub versions) / *Sleeping Angel / Edge Of Seventeen (Live)

LOVES A HARD GAME TO PLAY

U.S. Release Date: November 1991
Catalogue Number:
U.K. Release Date: Not Released
Catalogue Number:
Producer. *Bret Michaels / #Jimmy Iovine
Tracks: *Loves A Hard Game To Play (Remix) / #Sleeping Angel (Remix)
U.S. Cassette single Modern 74-98662

REISSUES

SINGLES

Stop Draggin' My Heart Around / Leather And Lace
U.S. Atlantic 13236
U. K. Not Released

Nightbird / Anyone Falls
U.S. Atlantic 784998
U.K. Not Released

Stand Back / Edge Of Seventeen
U.S. Atlantic 13258
U.K. Not Released

Edge Of Seventeen / Leather And Lace
U.S. Modern MS 5785
U.K. Not Released

Talk To Me / I Can't Wait
U.S. Atlantic 784964
U.K. Not Released

STEVIE NICKS APPEARS ON

ALBUMS

WARREN ZEVON
WARREN ZEVON
U.S. Asylum 7E 1060 (1976)
U.K. Asylum K 53039 (1976)

TOM SNOW
TOM SNOW
U.S. Capitol ST 11545 (1976)
U.K. Not Released

WALTER EGAN
FUNDAMENTAL ROLL
U.S. CBS 34679 (1977)
U.K. Polydor 2310614 (1977)

WALTER EGAN
NOT SHY
U.S. CBS 3S077 (1978)
U.K. Polydor 231O609 (1977)

189

KENNY LOGGINS

NIGHTWATCH

U.S. Columbia JC 35387 (1978)

U.K. CBS 82865 (1978)

TODD RUNDGREN

BACK TO THE BARS

U.S. Bearsville 6986 (1978)

U.K. Bearsville K 65511 (1978)

DANE DONAHUE

DANE DONAHUE

U.S. Columbia JC 34278 (1978)

U.K. Not Released

JOHN STEWART

BOMBS AWAY DREAM BABIES

U.S. RSO RS 13051 (1979)

U.K. RSO 2394228 (1979)

BOB WELCH

THREE HEARTS

U.S. Capitol SO 11907 (1979)

U.K. Capitol EA-ST 11907 (1979)

TOM PETTY AND THE HEARTBREAKERS

HARD PROMISES

U.S. Backstreet 5160 (1981)

U.K. MCA MCF 3098 (1981)

LOUISE GOFFIN

LOUISE GOFFIN

U.S. Asylum 6E 333 (1981)

U.K.

ROBBIE PATTON

ORDERS FROM HEADQUARTERS

U.S. Atlantlc 80006 - 1 (1982)

U.K. Atlantic 7800061 (1982)

SANDY STEWART

CATDANCER

U.S. Modern 90133 - 1 (1984)

U.K. Not Released

TOM PETTY AND THE HEARTBREAKERS

PACK UP THE PLANTATION LIVE

U.S. MCA LP 8021 (1985)

U.K. MCA MCMD 7001 (1985)

VARIOUS ARTISTS

A VERY SPECIAL CHRISTMAS

U.S. A&M / SOL 3911 (1987)

U.K.

WILLIAMS BROTHERS

TWO STORIES

U.S. Warner Brothers 25547 (1987)

U. K.

Note: Stevie Nicks wrote one track-You Like Me

MARIA VIDAL

MARIA VIDAL

U.S. A&M SP6-5160 (1987)

U.K. Not Released

B.B. KING

KING OF THE BLUES 1989

U.S. MCA 42183 (1989)

U.K.

RICK VITO

KING OF HEARTS

U.S. Modern Records 7 - 91789 (1992)

U.K.

S0UNDTRACKS

VARIOUS ARTISTS

HEAVY METAL

U.S. Full Moon / Asylum DP 90004 (1981)

U.K. Epic EPC 88558 (1981)

VARIOUS ARTISTS

FAST TIMES AT RIDGEMONT HIGH

U.S. Full Moon / Asylum 60158 (1981)

U.K. WEA K99246 (1981)

VARIOUS ARTISTS

AGAINST ALL ODDS

U.S. Atlantic 81052 (1984)

U.K. Virgin VC 2313 (1984)

VARIOUS ARTISTS

STREETS QF FIRE

U.S. MCA 5492 (1984)

U.K.

Note: Stevie wrote one song - Sorcerer

VARIOUS ARTISTS

WHITE NIGHTS

U.S. Atlantic 7-89498 (1985)

U. K.

VARIOUS ARTISTS

AMERICAN ANTHEM

U.S. Atlantic 81661 (1986)

U.K.

SINGLES

WARREN ZEVON

Hasten Down The Wind / Mohammid's Radio

U.S. Asylum K 5356 (1976)

U.K. Not Released

WARREN ZEVON

I'll Sleep When I'm Dead / Mohammid's Radio

U.S. Not Released

U.K. Asylum K 10360 (1976)

WALTER EGAN

Only The Lucky / I'd Rather Have Fun

U.S. CBS 10531 (1977)

U.K. United Artists UP 36245 (1977)

WALTER EGAN

When I Get My Wheels / Waitin'

U.S. CBS 310591 (1977)

U.K. United Artists UP 36321 (1977)

WALTER EGAN

Sweet South Breeze / Tunnel O'Love

U.S. Not Released

U.K. Polydor 2001807 (1978)

WALTER EGAN

Magnet And Steel / She's So Tough

U.S. Not Released

U.K. Polydor 2001807 (1978)

WALTER EGAN

Magnet And Steel / Only The Lucky

U.S. Columbia 3 - 10719 (1978)

U.K. Not Released

KENNY LOGGINS

Whenever I Call You Friend / Angelique

U.S. Columbia 3 - 10794 (1978)

U.K. CBS 6551 (1978)

JOHN STEWART

Gold / Comin' Out Of Nowhere

U.S. RS0 931 (1979)

U.K. RS0 35 (1979)

JOHN STEWART

Midnight Wind / Comin' Out Of Nowhere

U.S. RSO RS 1000 (1979)

U.K. RSO 42 (1979)

TOM PETTY AND THE HEARTBREAKERS

Insider / A Woman In Love (It's Not Me)

U.S. MCA MCS 10334 (1981)

U.K. Not Released

TOM PETTY AND THE HEARTBREAKERS

Insider / Refugee

U.S. Not Released

U.K. MCA 778 (1981)

U.K. Limited Edition picture disk single MCAP 778

ROBBIE PATTON

Smiling Islands / Feel The Flow

U.S. Atlantic 7-89955 (1982)

U.K.

SANDY STEWART

Saddest Victory / Mind Over Matter

U.S. Modern 7 - 99774 (1984)

U.K. Not Released

TOM PETTY AND THE HEARTBREAKERS

Needles And Pins / Spike

U.S. MCA MCA 52772 (1985)

U.K. Not Released

MARILYN MARTIN AND PHIL COLLINS

Seperate Lives / I Don't Wanna Know

U.S. Atlantic 7-89498 (1985)

U. K.

BLUE YONDER

Wind Song / Only For A Moment

U.S.

U.K.

STEVIE NICKS VIDEOS

LIVE IN CONCERT

U.S. CBS FOX 7136 (1983)

U.K. CBS FOX 713650 (1983)

Tracks: Gold Dust Woman / Golden Braid / I Need To Know/ Dreams / Stop Draggin' My Heart Around / Sara / Edge Of Seventeen / Outside The Rain / Rhiannon.

RED ROCKS

U.S. Sony R0650BEB (1987)

U.K. Castle Hendering HEN 2062G (1987)

Tracks: Outside The Rain / Dreams / Talk To Me / I Need To / No Spoken Word / Beauty And The Beast / Stand Back / Has Anyone Ever Written Anything For You / Edge Of Seventeen.

I CAN'T WAIT

U.S. RCA Columbia 60524 (1986)

U.K. RCA RVT 10794 (1986)

Tracks: Stop Draggin' My Heart Around / Stand Back / Leather And Lace / If Anyone Falls / Talk To me / I Can't Wait.

STEVIE NICKS GUESTS ON

VARIOUS ARTISTS

WOMEN IN ROCK

U.S.

U.K. Virgin VIR 175 2 (1987)

TOM PETTY AND THE HEARTBREAKERS

A BUNCH OF VIDEOS AND S0ME OTHER STUFF

U.S. MPI Home Entertainment MP 1668 (1989)

U.K.

VIDEO / LASERDISK

STEVIE NICKS GUESTS ON

BOB WELCH

BOB WELCH AND FRIENDS LIVE AT THE ROXY

U.S. Select a Vision / RCA Records Laserdisk (1982)

U.K. Not Released

CHRISTINE McVIE DISCOGRAPHY PRIOR TO JOINING FLEETWOOD MAC

CHRISTINE (PERFECT) McVIE ALBUMS

CHRISTINE PERFECT

U.S. Release Date: Not Released

Catalogue Number:

U.K. Release Date: June 1970

Catalogue Number: Blue Horizon 7-63860

Producer: Mike Vernon / Christine Perfect

*Danny Kirwan

Tracks: Crazy'Bout You / I'm On My Way / Let Me Go (Leave Me Alone) / Wait And See / Close To Me / I'd Rather Go Blind / *When You Say / And That's Saying A Lot / No Road Is The Right Road / For You / I'm Too Far Gone (To Turn Around) / I Want You.

Reissue: U.K. CBS 32198 (1982) Note: Different cover

CHRISTINE (PERFECT) McVIE SINGLES

I'D RATHER GO BLIND

U.S. Release Date: June 1969

Catalogue Number: Blue Horizon 300

U.K. Release Date: Not Released

Catalogue Number:

Producer: Mike Vernon / Christine Perfect

Tracks: I'd Rather Go Blind / Close To Me

WHEN YOU SAY

U.S. Release Date: Not Released

Catalogue Number:

U.K. Release Date: October 1969

Catalogue Number: Blue Horizon 57-3165

Producer: Danny Kirwan

Tracks: When You Say / No Road Is The Right Road

I'M TOO FAR GONE (TO TURN AROUND)

U.S. Release Date: Not Released

Catalogue Number:

U.K. Release Date: April 1970

Catalogue Number: Blue Horizon 57 - 3172

Producer: Mike Vernon / Christine Perfect

Tracks: I'm Too Far Gone (To Turn Around) / Close To Me

CHRISTINE McVIE APPEARS ON

ALBUMS

CHICKEN SHACK

FOURTY BLUE FINGERS FRESHLY PACKED AND READY TO SERVE

U.S. Epic BN 26414 (1968)

U.K. Blue Horizon 7-63203 (1968)

CHICKEN SHACK

O.K. KEN?

U.S. Blue Horizon BH 7705 (1968)

U.K. Blue Horizon 7-63209 (1968)

FLEETWOOD MAC

MR. WONDERFUL

U.S. Not Released

U.K. Blue Horizon 7-63205 (1968)

FLEETWOOD MAC

ENGLISH ROSE

U.S. Epic BN 26446 (1969)

U.K. Not Released

MARTHA VELEZ

FIENDS AND ANGELS

U.S. Sire 97008 (1969)

U.K. Blue Horizon 7-63867 (1969)

SINGLES

CHICKEN SHACK

It's Ok With Me Baby / When My left Eye Jumps

U.S. Not Released

U.K. Blue Horizon 57-31135 (1967)

CHICKEN SHACK

Worried About My Woman / Six Nights In Seven

U.S. Epic 10414 (1968

U.K. Blue Horizon 57-3143 (1968)

CHICKEN SHACK

When The Train Comes Back / Hey Baby

U.S. Not Released

U.K. Blue Horizon 57-3146 (1968)

FLEETWOOD MAC

Need Your Love So Bad / Stop Messin'Round

U.S. Not Released

U.K. Blue Horizon 57-3139 (1968)

FLEETWOOD MAC

Need Your Love So Bad / No Place To Go

U.S. Epic 5-10386 (1968)

U.K. Blue Horizon 57 -3157 (1968)

CHICKEN SHACK

I'd Rather Go Blind / Night Life

U.S. Not Released

U.K. Blue Horizon 57-3153 (1969)

CHICKEN SHACK

I'd Rather Go Blind / Get Like You Used To Be

U.S. Epic 10536 (1969)

U.K. Not Released

MARTHA VELEZ

It Takes A Lot To Laugh,It Takes A Train To Cry / Come Here Sweet Man

U.S. Sire U 10266 (1969)

U.K. Not Released

MARTHA VELEZ

Tell Mama / Swamp Man

U.S. Sire K 10280 (1969)

U.K. Not Released

COMPILATION AND REISSUE ALBUMS

CHRISTINE McVIE

THE LEGENDARY CHRISTINE PERFECT

U.S. Sire SR 6022 (1976)

U.S. Reissue Sire SASD 7552 (1977)

U.K. Not Released

Note: Reissue of Christine Perfect U.K. Blue Horizon 7-63860

CHICKEN SHACK

GOLDEN ERA OF POP MUSIC

U.S. Not Released

U.K. CBS 68252 (1977)

FLEETWOOD MAC / CHRISTINE PERFECT

ALBATROSS

U.S. Not Released

U.K. Embassy S CBS 31569 (1977)

Note: Side two Christine Perfect

FLEETWOOD MAC

GREATEST HITS

CHICKEN SHACK

IN THE CAN

U.S. Not Released

U.K. CBS 31811 (1980)

CHICKEN SHACK

THE COLLECTOR SERIES

U.S. Not Released

U.K. Castle Communications CCSLP 179 (1988)

REISSUE SINGLES

CHICKEN SHACK

I'd Rather Go Blind / Tears In The Wind

U.S. CBS Old Gold 9201 (1982)

U.K. Not Released

CHICKEN SHACK

I'd Rather Go Blind / Sad Clown

U.S. Not Released

U.K. CBS 1832 (1974)

CHRISTINE McVIE DISCOGRAPHY

CHRISTINE McVIE ALBUMS

CHRISTINE McVIE

U.S. Release Date February 1984

Catalogue Number: Warner Brothers 25059- 1

U.K. Release Date: February 1984

Producer: Russ Titelman

Tracks: Love Will Show Us How / The

Challenge / So Excited / One In A Million / Ask

Anybody / Got A Hold On Me / Who's Dreaming

This Dream / I'm The One / Keeping Secrets /

The Smile I Live For

U.S. CD Warner Brothers 25059-2 (1984)

U.K. CD Warner Brothers 925059-2 (1984)

CHRISTINE McVIE SINGLES

GOT A HOLD ON ME

U.S. Release Date: January 1984

Catalogue Number: Warner Brothers 7- 29372

U.K. Release Date February 1984

Catalogue Number: Warner Brothers W 9372

Producer: Russ Titelman

Tracks: Got A Hold On Me / Who's Dreaming

This Dream

U.K. 12" single Warner Brothers W 9372PT

Limited Edition picture disk Got A Hold On Me /

Who's Dreaming This Dream

LOVE WILL SHOW US HOW

U.S. Release Date: April 1984

Catalogue Number: Warner Brothers 7-29313

U.K. Release Date: April 1984

Catalogue Number: Warner Brothers W 93 1 3

Producer: Russ Titelman

Tracks: The Challenge / I'm The One

THE CHALLENGE

U.S. Release Date: September 1984

Catalogue Number: Warner Brothers 7 - 29160

U.K Release Date: Not Released

Catalogue Number:

Producer: Russ Titelman

Tracks: The Challenge / I'm The One

REISSUES

SINGLES

Got A Hold On Me / Love Will Show Us How

U.S. Warner Brothers GWB 0988

U.K. Not Released

CHRISTINE McVIE APPEARS ON

ALBUMS

BOB WELCH

FRENCH KISS

U.S. Capitol EST 11663 (1977)

U.K. Capitol CL 15951 (1977)

BOB WELCH

THREE HEARTS

U.S. Capitol SO 11907 (1979)

U.K. Capitol EA-ST 11907 (1979)

JOHN STEWART

BOMBS AWAY DREAM BABIES

U.S. RSO RS 13051 (1979)

U.K. RSO 2394228 (1979)

DANNY DOUMA

NIGHT EYES

U.S. Warner Brothers 3326 (1979)

U.K. Not Released

LINDSEY BUCKINGHAM

LAW AND ORDER

U.S.Asylum SE 561 (1981)

U.K. Mercury 6302 167 (1981)

ROBBIE PATTON

DISTANT SHORES

U.S. LibertyLT 1107 (1981)

U.K. Not Released

ROBBIE PATTON

ORDERS FROM HEADQUARTERS

U.S. Atlantic 800O6- 1 (1982)

U.K. Atlantic 78OO061 (1982)

WALTER EGAN

WILD EXHIBITIONS

U.S. Backstreet BSR 5400 (1983)

U.K.

RANDY NEWMAN

TROUBLE IN PARIDISE

U.S. Warner Brothers 23755 (1983)

U.K. Warner Brothers W 3755 (1983)

MICK FLEETWOOD'S ZOO

I'M NOT ME

U.S. RCA 4652 (1983)

U.K. RCA PL 84652 (1983)

BILLY BURNETTE

TRY ME

U.S. MCA / Curb MCA 5604 (1985)

U.K.

TODD SHARP

WHO AM I

U.S. MCA 5579 (1986)

U.K. Not Released

BONNIE RAITT

NINE LIVES

U.S. Warner Brathers 25685 (1986)

U.K. Warner Brothers 9254861 1986)

CHRISTOPHER CROSS

BACK OF MY MIND

U.S. Warner Brothers 25685 (1988)

U.K. Warner Brothers WX 158 (1988)

VARIOUS ARTISTS COMPILATION

ROCK, RHYTHM & BLUES

U.S. Warner Brothers 1 -25817 (1989)

U.K. WEA WX 255 (1989)

SOUNDTRACK

VARIOUS ARTISTS

A FINE MESS

U.S. Motown (1986)

U.K. Motown (1986)

SINGLES

BOB WELCH

Sentimental Lady / Hot Love, Cold World

U.S. Capitol 4479 (1977)

U.K. Capitol CL 15970 (1978)

BOB WELCH

Church / Don't Wait Too Long

U.S. Capitol P 4719 (1979)

U.K. Capitol CL 16086 (1979)

BOB WELCH

Precious Love / Something Strong

U.S. Capitol 4685 (1979)

U.K. Capitol CL 16070 (1979)

ROBBIE PATTON

Don't Give It Up / When Love Disappears

U.S. Liberty 1420 (1981)

U.K. Not Released

RANDY NEWMAN

I Love L.A. / Song For The Dead

U.S. Warner Brothers 7-29687 (1983)

U.K. Warner Brothers 9687 (1983)

BILLY BURNETTE

It Ain't Over /

U.S. MCA 52710 (1985)

U. K. Not Released

CHRISTINE McVIE VIDEOS

CHRISTINE McVIE - THE VIDEO ALBUM

U.S. Vestron Music MA 1013 (1984)

U.K. Vestron 21013 CHRM 1 (1984)

Tracks: Love Will Show Us How / Keeping

Fleetwood Mac

BEHIND THE MASK

Secrets / The Challenge / Who's Dreaming
This Dream / I'm The One / So Excited / Got A
Hold On Me / One In A Million / You Make
Loving Fun / Don't Stop / World Turning /
Songbird

CHRISTINE McVIE APPEARS ON

VIDEOS

VARIOUS ARTISTS
WOMEN IN ROCK
U.S.
U.K. Virgin VIR 175 2 (1987)

JOHN McVIE DISCOGRAPHY

JOHN McVIE ALBUMS

**JOHN McVIE'S "GOTTA BAND" WITH
LOLA THOMAS**
U.S. Release Date: May 1992
Catalogue Number: Warner Brothers 26909
U.K. Release Date: May 1992
Catalogue Number: WEA 26909
Producer: John McVie / Dennis Walker
Tracks: Evidence / Now I Know / Lost What
You Had / Shot Down By Love / Step Aside /
You Left Me Lonely / The Bigger The Love /
All That In Was Guilty Of... / One More Time
With Feeling / The Way I Do.
U.S. CD Warner Brothers 9 26909 2 (1992)
U.K. CD WEA 26909 2 (1992)

JOHN McVIE SINGLES

NOW I KNOW
U.S. Release Date: July 1992
Catalogue Number: Warner Brothers 4-18841
U.K. Release Date: Not Released
Catalogue Number:
Producer: John McVie / Dennis Walker
Tracks: Now I Know / One More Time With
Feeling

JOHN McVIE APPEARS ON

ALBUMS

EDDIE BOYD
7936 SOUTH RHODES

U.S. Not Released
U.K. Blue Horizon 7-63202 (1968)

DUSTER BENNETT
SMILING LIKE I'M HAPPY
U.S. Not Released
U.K. Blue Horizon 7-63208 (1968)

GORDON SMITH
LONG OVERDUE
U.S. Not Released
U.K. Blue Horizon 7 - 63211 (1968)

OTIS SPANN
THE BIGGEST THING SINCE COLOSSUS
U.S. Blue Horizon 4802 (1969)
U.K. Blue Horizon 7-63217 (1969)

CHRISTINE PERFECT
CHRISTINE PERFECT
U.S. Not Released
U.K. Blue Horizon 7-63860 (1970)

JEREMY SPENCER
JEREMY SPENCER
U.S. Not Released
U.K. Reprise RSLP 9002 (1970)

JOHN MAYALL
BANQUET IN BLUES
U.S. ABC ABCD 958 (1975)
U.K. ABC ABCL 5187 (1976)

WARREN ZEVON
EXCITABLE BOY
U.S. Asylum 6E 118 (1978)
U.K. Asylum K 53973 (1978)

ROBERT FLEISCHMAN
PERFECT STRANGER
U.S. Arista AB4220 (1979)
U.K. Not Released

ROB GRILL
UPROOTED
U.S. Mercury SMR 13798 (1979)
U.K. Mercury 9111055 (1979)

DANNY DOUMA
NIGHT EYES
U S Warner Brothers 3326 (1979)
U.K. Not Released

SOUNDTRACK
A FINE MESS
U.S. Motown (1986)
U.K. Motown (1986)

VARIOUS ARTISTS COMPILATION
ROCK , RHYTHM & BLUES
U.S. Warner Brothers 1 -25817 (1989)
U.K. WEA WX 255 (1989)

SINGLES

EDDIE BOYD
The Big Boat / Sent For You Yesterday
U.S. Not Released
U.K. Blue Horizon 57-3137 (1968)

DUSTER BENNETT
It's A Man Down There / Things Are Changing
U.S. Not Released
U.K. Blue Horizon 57-4141 (1968)

OTIS SPANN
Walkin' / Temperature Is Rising (98.8)
U.S. Not Released
U.K. Blue Horizon 57 -3155 (1969)

OTIS SPANN
Hungry Country Girl / Walkin'
U.S. Blue Horizon 304 (1969)
U.K. Not Released

CHRISTINE PERFECT
When You Say / No Road Is The Right Road
U.S. Not Released
U.K. Blue Horizon 57-3165 (1969)

CLIFFORD DAVIS
Before The Beginning / Man Of The World
U.S. Not Released
U.K. Reprise RS 27003 (1969)

CLIFFORD DAVIS
Come On Down And Follow Me / Homework

U.S. Not Released
U.K. Reprise 27008 (1970)

JEREMY SPENCER
Linda / Teenage Darling
U.S. Not Released
U.K. Reprise RS 27002 (1969)

CLIFFORD DAVIS
Man Of The World / Before The Beginning
U.S. Not Released
U.K. Reprise K 14282 (1973)

WARREN ZEVON
Werewolves Of London / Roland The Headless
Thompson Gunner
U.S. Asylum E 45472A (1978)
U.K. Asylum K 13111 (1978)
U.S. 12" single Asylum 11386 Limited Edition
picture disk Werewolves Of London / Roland
The Headless Thompson Gunner

ROB GRILL
Rock Suger / Have Mercy
U.S. Mercury 76009 (1979)
U.K. Mercury 6167 836 (1980)

AUSSIE BAND
Somebody Wants You / Cry Your Life Away
U.S. Real World RW 7309 (1980)
U.K. Not Released

JOHN McVIE APPEARS ON

VIDEO / LASERDISK

BOB WELCH
BOB WELCH AND FRIENDS LIVE AT THE
ROXY
U.S. Select A Vision / RCA Records Laserdisk
(1982)
U.K. Not Released

VIDEOS

JOHN MAYALL'S BIUESBREAKERS
THE BLUES ALIVE
U.S.
U.K. RCA RVT 10377 (1984)

MICK FLEETWOOD DISCOGRAPHY

MICK FLEETWOOD ALBUMS

THE VISITOR

U.S. Release Date: June 1981

Catalogue Number: RCA AFL 14080

U.K. Release Date: June 1981

Catalogue Number: RCA RCALP 5044

Producer: Richard Dashut / Mick Fleetwood

Tracks: Rattlesnake Shake / You Weren't In
love / O'Niamali / Super Brains / Don't Be
Sorry, Just Be Happy / Walk A Thin Line / Not
Fade Away / Cassiopeia Surrender / The Visitor
/ Amelle (Come On Show Me Your Heart).

Reissue: U.K. BMG PIPLP 020

U.S. CD Not Released

U.K. CD BMG PIPCD 020

MICK FLEETWOOD'S ZOO

I'M NOT ME

U.S. Release Date: September 1983

Catalogue Number. RCA 4652

U.K. Release Date: November 1983

Catalogue Number: RCA PL 84652

Producer: Richard Dashut / Mick Fleetwood

Tracks: Angel Come Home / You Might Need
Somebody / Tonight / I Want You Back / I'm
Not Me / State Of The Art / Tear It Up / This
Love / I Give / Just Because / Put Me Right.

THE ZOO

SHAKIN' THE CAGE

U.S. Release Date: June 1992

Catalogue Number: Capricorn 42004

U.K. Release Date:

Catalogue Number:

Producer: Billy Thorpe / Mick Fleetwood

Tracks: Reach Out / God Created Woman /
Nightlife / Shakin' The Cage / Voodoo / How
Does It Feel / The Night And You / Takin' It
Out To The People / Breakin' Up / In Your Hands.

MICK FLEETWOOD SINGLES

YOU WEREN'T IN LOVE

U.S. Release Date: August 1981

Catalogue Number: RCA PB 12308

U.K. Release Date: August 1981

Catalogue Number: RCA 118

Producer: Richard Dashut / Mick Fleetwood

Tracks: You Weren't In Love / O' Niamali

MICK FLEETWOOD'S ZOO

I WANT YOU BACK

U.S. Release Date: September 1983

Catalogue Number. RCA PB - 3621

U.K. Release Date: October 1983

Catalogue Number: RCA 360

Producer: Richard Dashut / Mick Fleetwood

Tracks: I Want You Back / Put Me Right

THE ZOO

SHAKIN'THE CAGE

U.S. Release Date: Not Released

Catalogue Number:

U.K. Release Date: Not Released

Catalogue Number:

Producer: Billy Thorpe

Tracks: Shakin'The Cage / Forgive

Note: Released only in Australia on March 18th
1991

7 " single Mushroom K 10370

Cassette single Mushroom C 10370

CD single Mushroom D 10370

THE ZOO

SHAKIN' THE CAGE

U.S. Release Date: May 1992

Catalogue Number: Capricorn 4 - 18920

U.K. Release Date:

Catalogue Number:

Producer: Billy Thorpe / Mick Fleetwood

Tracks: Shakin' The Cage / Takin' It To The
People

MICK FLEETWOOD APPEARS ON

ALBUMS

EDDIE BOYD

7936 SOUTH RHODES

U.S. Not Released

U.K. Blue Horizon 7-63202 (1968)

DUSTER BENNETT

SMILING LIKE I'M HAPPY

U.S. Not Released

U.K. Blue Horizon 7-63208 (1968)

GORDON SMITH

LONG OVERDUE

U.S. Not Released

U.K. Blue Horizon 7-63211 (1968)

TRAMP

TRAMP

U.S. Not Released

U.K. Music Man 603 (1969)

JEREMY SPENCER

JEREMY SPENCER

U.S. Not Released

U.K. Reprise RSLP 9002 (1970)

ALVIN LEE & MYLON LE FEVRE

ON THE ROAD TO FREEDOM

U.S. DBS 32729 (1973)

U.K. Chrysalis 1054 (1973)

TRAMP

PUT A RECORD ON

U.S. Not Released

U.K. Spark SLRP 112 (1974)

BOB WELCH

FRENCH KISS

U.S. Capitol EST 1166S (1977)

U.K. Capitol CL 15951 (1977)

WARREN ZEVON

EXCITABLE BOY

U.S. Asylum 6E 118 (1978)

U.K. Asylum K53973 (1978)

WALTER EGAN

NOT SHY

U.S. Columbia JC 35077 (1978)

U.K. Polydor 2310609 (1978)

BOB WELCH

THREE HEARTS

U.S. Capitol SO 11907 (1979)

U.K. Capltol EA-ST 11907 (1979)

RON WOOD

GIMME SOME NECK

U.S. CBS 35702 (1979)

U.K. CBS 83337 (1979)

DANNY DOUMA

NIGHT EYES

U.S. Warner Brothers 3326 (1979)

U.K. Not Released

ROB GRILL

UPROOTED

U.S. Mercury 9RM 13798 (1979)

U.K. Mercury 9111055 (1979)

TURLEY RICHARDS

THERFU

U.S. Atlantic 19260 (1980)

U.K. Not Released

LINDSEY BUCKINGHAM

LAW AND ORDER

U.S. Mercury 5E 561 (1981)

U.K. Mercury 630 2167 (1981)

STEVIE NICKS

THE WILD HEART

U.S. Atco 90084 - 1 (1983)

U.K. WEA 2500711 (1983)

CHRISTINE McVIE

CHRISTINE McVIE

U.S. Warner Brothers 25059 (1984)

U.K. Warner Brothers 9250291 (1984)

BILLY BURNETTE

U.S. MCA / Curb MCA 5604 (1985)

U.K.

JIMMY BARNES

JIMMY BARNES

U.S. Geffen GHS 24089 (1985)

U.K.

SOUNDTRACK

A FINE MESS

U.S. Motown (1986)

U.K. Motown (1986)

PETE BARDENS

SPEED OF LIGHT

U.S.Capitol CI-48967(1988)

U.K. Capitol EST 2076 (1989)

B.B. KING

KING OF THE BLUES 1989

U.S. MCA 42183 (1989)

U.K. MCA MCG 6038 (1989)

VARIOUS ARTISTS COMPILATION

ROCK, RHYTHM & BLUES

U.S. Warner Brothers 1-25817 (1989)

U.K. WEA WX255 (1989)

PAUL SHAFFER

COAST TO COAST

U.S. Capitol 005784 (1989)

U.K.

SINGLES

EDDIE BOYD

The Big Boat / Sent For You Yesterday

U.S. Not Released

U.K. Blue Horizon 57-3137 (1968)

DUSTER BENNETT

It's A Man Down There / Things Are Changeing

U.S. Not Released

U.K. Blue Horizon 57 -3141 (1968)

OTIS SPANN

Hungry Country Girl / Walkin'

U.S. Blue Horizon 304 (1969)

U.K. Not Released

CLIFFORD DAVIS

Before The Beginning / Man Of The World

U.S. Not Released

U.K. Reprise RS 27003 (1969)

CLIFFORD DAVIS

Come On Down And Follow Me / Homework

U.S. Not Released

U.K. Reprise 27008 (1970)

JEREMY SPENCER

Linda / Teenage Darling

U.S. Not Released

U.K. Reprise RS 27002 (1969)

CLIFFORD DAVIS

Man Of The World / Before The Beginning

U.S. Not Released

U.K. Reprise K 14282 (1973)

ALVIN LEE AND MYLON LE FEVRE

So Sad (No Love Of His Own) / Riffin'

U.S. Columbia 45987 (1973)

U.K. Chrysalis CHS 2035 (1974)

BOB WELCH

Sentimental Lady / Hot Love,Cold World

U.S. Capitol 4479 (1978)

U.K. Capitol CL 15970 (1978)

WARREN ZEVON

Werewolves Of London / Roland The Headless
Thompson Gunner

U.S. Asylum E 454 72A (1978)

U.K. Asylum K 13111 (1978)

U.S. 12" Picture Disk Asylum 11386 (1978)

DANNY DOUMA

Hate You /

U.S. Warner Brothers WBS 4910 (1979)

U.K. Not Released

BOB WELCH

Precious Love / Something Strong

U.S. Capitol 4685 (1979)

U.K. Capitol CL 16070 (1979)

BOB WELCH

Church / Don't Wait Too Long

U.S. Capitol P4719 (1979)

U.K. Capitol CL 16086 (1979)

RON WOOD

Seven Days / Breakin' My Heart

U.S. Columbia 311014 (1979)

U.K. Not Released

RON WOOD

Seven Days / Come To Realise

U.S. Not Released

U.K. CBS 7785 (1979)

ROB GRILL

Rock Sugar / Have Mercy

U.S. Mercury 76009 (1980)

U.K. Mercury 6167 836 (1980)

TURLEY RICHARDS

You MIght Need Somebody / It's All Up To You

U.S. Atlantic 3664 (1980)

U.K.

TURLEY RICHARDS

Stand By Me /

U.S. Atlantic 3660 (1980)

U.K.

LINDSEY BUCKINGHAM

Trouble / That's How We Do It In L.A.

U.S. Not Released

U.K. Mercury MER 85 (1981)

LINDSEY BUCKINGHAM

Trouble / Mary Lee Jones

U.S. Asylum 47223 (1981)

U.K. Not Released

B.B.KING

Standing On The Edge Of Love / Don't Tell
Me Nothing

U.S.

U.K. MCA 1124 (1988)

U.K. 12" single MCA T1124(1988)

PETE BARDENS

Whisper In The Wind /

U.S.

U.K.

VARIOUS ARTISTS

SplrIt Of The Forest / Spirit Of The Forest

U.S.

U.K. Virgin VS 1191 (1989)

U.S. 12" single Virgin 096551 (1989)

U.K. 12" single

COMPILATION AND REISSUE ALBUMS

THE SHOTGUN EXPRESS

E.P. 10"

U.S. Not Released

U.K. Charly CYM 2 (1983)

Tracks: Side 1, I Could Feel The Whole World
Turn 'Round / Curtains

Side 2, Funny 'Cos Neither Could I / Indian
Thing

LASERDISK

MICK FLEETWOOD

THE VISITOR

U.S. RCA 02125 (1982)

U.K. Not Released

Tracks: Not Fade Away / O'Niamali / Ebaali
Gbiko Folksong / Walk A ThIn Line / You
Weren't In Love / John Lennen Tribute / The
Visitor / Rattlesnake Shake / Ebaali Folksong
(Reprise) / O'Niamali(Reprise)

Shake Your Moneymaker / Not Fade Away
(Reprise)

MICK FLEETWOOD APPEARS ON

BOB WELCH

BOB WELCH AND FRIENDS LIVE AT THE
ROXY

U.S. Select a vision / RCA Records Laserdisk
(1982)

U.K. Not Released

VIDEOS

MICK FLEETWOOD APPEARS ON

STEVIE NICKS

RED ROCKS

U.S. Sony R0650BEB (1987)

U.K. Castle Hendering HEN 2062G (1987)

CHRISTINE McVIE

CHRISTINE McVIE-THE VIDEO ALBUM

U.S. Vestron Music MA 1013 (1984)

U.K, Vestron 21013 CHRM 1 (1984)

199

PHOTOGRAPHY CREDITS

RICHARD ARMAS
p.125–all

PETER BEARD
Dedication page

RICHARD DASHUT
p.122-123–all

DENNIS DUNSTAN
p.133

SAM EMERSON
p.44–bottom, p.62, p.64-67, p.78-79,
p.80–top, p.80–bottom, p.81–top right,
p.81–bottom right, p.82, p.83, p.90,
p.91–top, p.91–bottom, p.92-93, p.105–top,
p.105–bottom, p.108-111, p.112–top right,
p.115, p.119, p.124, p.127, p.128–top right,
p.128–bottom left, p.128–bottom right,
p.132, p.134–all

MICK FLEETWOOD
title page (self portrait) p.29, p.36, p.45,
p.58, p.84–top, p.84–bottom, p.86–all

AMY FLEETWOOD
p.201

EDDIE GARRICK
p.72, p.73–top left

RICHARD GITLIN
p.145–top left, p.145–bottom

RANDALL HAGADORN
p.71–bottom left, p.88, p.96-103–all, p.106-
107, p.112–bottom right, p.126, Back cover

TERENCE IBBOTT
p.8–above, p.8–below, p.9, p.17–above,
p.19, p.23-24, p.42-43, p.44–above, p.46, p.47

JOHN McVIE
p.10-11, p.14, p.16, p.17–bottom, p.18–top,
p.18–bottom, p.28, p.32-33, p.36–top, p.37-
38, p.56, p.59-60

BILL DARAS PAUSTENBACH
p.69, p.70, p.71–top, p.71–bottom right,
p.113, p.146–all

NEAL PRESTON
p.81–middle right, p.95, p.114, p.128–top
middle, p.135, p.138-139, p.141, p.145–top
right, p.147

AARON RAPAPORT
p.136–left, p.136–right, p.137

TONY REAY
p.20

KEN REGAN / CAMERA 5
p.81–left

JIM SHEA
p.120, p.130-131

ANDY SILVESTER
p.50

SHARON WEISZ
p.73–bottom left, p.73–right, p.85, p.89,
p.94, p.104, p.112–top left, p.112–bottom
left, p.128–top left

MARK WRIGHT
p.30

TONY WYATT
p.12

p.VI Courtesy of Mick Fleetwood archive.
p.2-3 Courtesy of Peter Greenbaum family.
p.4-5 & p.21 Courtesy of Bob Brunning.
p.8–center Courtesy of Frank Harding collection.
p.25 Courtesy of Dave Elliot collection.
p.26 Courtesy of Michael Ochs Archive Ltd.
Venice, CA.
p.34 © 1971 Bill Graham #270, Artist: Pierre.
p.48 Courtesy of Disc from the Judy Wong
collection.
p.49 Courtesy of New Musical Express from
the Judy Wong collection.
p.61 Courtesy of Michael Ochs Archives Ltd.
Venice, CA. Photography by Michael Montfort.
p.74-75 Courtesy of Biddy Fleetwood.
p.76-77 Courtesy of Billboard Magazine.
p.116-117 Rolling Stone covers courtesy of
Straight Arrow Publishers Inc.
Photography by Annie Leibovitz–Rolling
Stone #235 3/24/77.
Photography by Annie Leibovitz–Rolling
Stone #256 1/12/78.
Photography by Richard Avedon–Rolling
Stone #310 2/7/80.
p.118 Courtesy of the Larry Vigon collection.
p.129 Courtesy of Wayne Cody.
p.142-144 Courtesy of Edinburgh Evening News.
p.144 Courtesy of Billy & Chris Burnette.
Discography: Albums courtesy of Warner
Brothers Records.